THE BOROUGHS

Hope you enjoy,

THE BOROUGHS

CRISTIAN VARGAS

NDP

NEW DEGREE PRESS
COPYRIGHT © 2021 CRISTIAN VARGAS
All rights reserved.

THE BOROUGHS

Disclaimer: This book contains the use of slang throughout at the writer's creative discretion and in no way reflects the editorial standards of the publisher.

ISBN	978-1-63676-485-6	*Paperback*
	978-1-63730-393-1	*Kindle Ebook*
	978-1-63730-394-8	*Ebook*

To all those that have helped me with this book from ideation to funding, writing, editing, and publishing. I want to specifically thank Isabella and Caleb for staying up till 4 a.m. every day for a whole week telling me my shit was trash and making sure it wasn't, though still insisting it was thereafter.

Ultimately, I want to thank me for not giving up and writing sixty thousand words through one of the hardest years of my adult life thus far. I say "thus far" because I know shit's just gonna go downhill from here.

TABLE OF CONTENTS

AUTHOR'S NOTE		11
CHAPTER 1.	THIS AIN'T ACADEMIA	15
CHAPTER 2.	FLACO, RAULI, AND PUERCO	27
CHAPTER 3.	A BUTTER ROLL	43
CHAPTER 4.	THE NEW YORKERS	59
CHAPTER 5.	A SUS REUNION	75
CHAPTER 6.	A RETROSPECTIVE WALK TO THE FUTURE	89
CHAPTER 7.	THE PINK HATS ARE EVERYWHERE	107
CHAPTER 8.	A COMIC'S THESIS	123
CHAPTER 9.	BALLAD OF THE TIRED BRETHREN	141
CHAPTER 10.	THE AESTHETIC OF HARD TRUTHS	157
CHAPTER 11.	YOU WON.	173
CHAPTER 12.	SOCKS	179
CHAPTER 13.	A FRUITFUL MISFORTUNE	185
CHAPTER 14.	RASTA MON IN THE BRONX	193
CHAPTER 15.	IT'S A CRAZY STORY	199
CHAPTER 16.	BEFORE AND AFTER	213
CHAPTER 17.	A LATE REALIZATION	225
EPILOGUE	#THEBOROUGHS	231
ACKNOWLEDGMENT		243

> "The only way you can know where the line is, is if you cross it."
>
> —DAVE CHAPPELLE

AUTHOR'S NOTE

"Don't go into that part of Brooklyn."

"The Bronx? The Bronx is dirty. Why would you even want to go above 103rd street?"

"Ew ... Staten Island." (Alright this one's kinda fair.)

I'm sure if you're from NYC you've heard these stereotypes and notions, some perpetuated jokingly by us, but seriously by others. Growing up in the encroaching gentrified Brooklyn, you're made to feel as if your only role is to be a cultural commodity to those who glorify "diversity" yet cast you aside. Your block is only cool once someone who doesn't look like you declares it so, takes all the substance, showcases it, and takes all the credit from you. You're made to feel subjugated by those who gentrify your block, call the cops on you, push you out, and—when trendy—hang their socially conscious flag outside their window. You're made to feel used by those who view your culture and pain as a convenient aesthetic, and not an inconvenient truth. This is a collective perspective that many people who live in New York experience and feel to different extents.

Hence, I wrote this book. *The Boroughs* is a portrayal of that inconvenient truth ... amongst other things.

Signs of resistance do not solely exist in protesting and boycotting, but also in creation. Creating something that cements us further into our existence, by virtue of our struggle and inspiration, is incumbent upon us as creators in times of great social distress. With those feelings in mind, I wanted to write something—ironically enough—that would add to the very **contemporary** culture of the city that people like me will never be prime benefactors of yet still continue to make ... because we love this city ... because at the end of the day, *we are* this city. This book is my contribution. This book is my testament. This book is my resistance.

There will be topics within this piece that will bother, challenge, and even offend you. Some things said and done **are not specifically my own personal vernacular, thoughts, or actions**, but are a representation of a culture that does use, or at least tolerates, said rhetoric and said actions. The truth is ... this is a nuanced perspective outside of what many may be used to, so please view this book with an open mind. While writing this book, I did a lot of soul-searching, talked to my fellow New Yorkers, and made peace with a lot of the strong emotions I had with writing this piece. I am aware of my faults and the ironic intersection of the topics described in this book. Like me, and many New Yorkers, the characters in this book have a lot of moral inconsistencies and flaws and—in the spirit of creating relatable and genuine characters—that *is* the point.

This book, apart from having serious topics, isn't an attempt at studying or portraying them, but more so a lashing out of perspective. It's not supposed to be taken literally or as a call for change. In fact, the book is mostly comedic and introspective. This book is also not an attempt at portraying New Yorkers—born and/or raised—as a monolith, but all those who grew up in the boroughs will find truths within it that will resonate heavily with them. To some readers it won't resonate, and if you read this book and realize you are one of *those* "New Yorkers," well ... welcome to the side you never ventured toward until it became trendy. I hope this reading is enlightening, for if you truly get it, the book itself is irony incarnate.

I put forth some of my most vulnerable thoughts and feelings, alongside the feelings of other New Yorkers, toward making this book. I am an amalgamation of all my experiences, and the experiences of those around me. I hope you enjoy my book, and that it inspires you to further the conversation and to contribute your story and your perspective to the collective NYC experience.

The Boroughs.

PS:
Before you continue reading, please google what satire is.

CHAPTER 1

THIS AIN'T ACADEMIA

―

JORDAN
[Ms. Jackson's Apartment]
[Brooklyn]
[9:48 a.m.]

"Communication has always been an important factor in war, but it had to be encrypted. Morse code being one of the"— The TV is turned off. Damn, shit was type interestin'.

"Dat damn channel has had dat show on repeat for a while now." Ms. Jackson rolls into the livin' room, remote in hand and reachin' for her big chair, she stops. "Jordan. Baby. You want sum to drink? Water?"

"Oh nah ... I'm—I'm good, Ms. Jackson."

Ms. Jackson waddles from side to side, holdin' the arm of the beaten, big chair for support. She plops down and lets out a wild chuckle as the floor creaks for help. Shorty fat as hell. I mean ... she's a *big* girl. Alex would kill me if she hears me callin' anyone fat. Wild breathin' in and out, swayin' forward and back, she rubs 'er chunky fingers on 'er legs while lookin' round the livin' room wide eyed. There's clothin' reachin' from all corners of the room, hidin' what I think is a bunch of old bitch shit. Old women love hoardin' shit. Lil angel figures, eighties church hats. As long as it takes up space, they'll keep it. Every surface the sun hit thru them bum ass curtains gives light to nothing but clothes on top of shit. The only object without stuff is a faded type of brown, scratched table in the middle of the room. Dust on top of the dried smudges of food, clearly from weeks ago, coats the table and … everythin', really.

Under the TV stand there's a bunch of faded pictures, its only shield Ms. Jackson's lack of hygiene, the dust barrier. I make the figures subtly and recognize no one in 'em. This livin' room dirty as hell. Right on the stand is the middle school graduation pic with Marcus's big ass forehead at the center. Shame on daddy for lettin' 'im go out like dat. Man, Marcus been ugly his whole life. No wonder he smart as hell, he gotta make up somehow. Growin' up, all the other kids would flame Marcus for his big ass forehead. He used to look at 'imself in the school bathroom mirror after we'd all roast 'im. I mean big forehead, big brains tho. Right beside dat picture was our high school grad pic. Barely visible, I look at a row of smilin' faces. Me, Abel, Marcus, and Alex, visibly cheesin' at the idea of finally leavin' high school, bein' adults, freedom, and a naive understandin' of it all. Little did we know, those days were gonna be our easiest and dat shit would never be the same. We weren't gonna be "free" or "movin' up" or whatever dumb shit we thought adulthood would bring us. Instead, all it brought was pain, distance from the things we love, and all the things our parents tried to shield us from. It's been nearly two years since dat first time we met up durin' winter break our first semester of college. We rarely have time to see each other, but today ... today is the day wh—

"Excuse the mess," Ms. Jackson says hymnally, while movin' clothin' to the side with 'er feet, slight dust kickin' up from 'er piles of clothes as she sways 'er chunk of a leg side to side, "I haven't been able to clean yet. I was just separating laundry today."

I cough and sneeze into my armpit, smile, and uncomfortably sit back on the plastic lined sofa next to a pile of white-stained clothes and random lingerie. Oh shit ... dat bra is helmet size. Nah lemme not look at dat before she gets the wrong idea. But damn bitch, you live like this? I've been up here before, and it's always been rough, but this is just some next level nasty type of shit. No wonder Marcus would sleep over often. I think I actually understand why he ain't get no pussy durin' high school. How you gon' bring shorty over to this nonsense. And he ain't bringin' no one to my crib and my room ... das a fact.

I look toward Ms. Jackson and wait for her to say sum. She doesn't. A still silence hits the room, as we nod and grin at each other awkwardly, bobbin' our heads back and forth. I look at 'er worn-down chair, with its seams and threads unravelin'. Dat shit look raggedy as fuck, but it looks way more comfortable than this. Why doesn't 'er chair got plastic? She prolly don't even have dat many people come over. I look down the dark hall toward Marcus's room. Man, I'on know what's takin' Marcus so long, but he better be comin' out quick. His auntie is ... off. She makin' me wild uncomfy. I thought this was an in and out situation. I'on know why— hol'up when was the last time she blinked? Ms. Jackson looks at me, her eyes slowly openin' wider, while crackin' a wide smile without showin' teeth. This bitch tweakin'. I nod and smile as I shift my eyes to look down the hall again. I look back to 'er. Still no blinkin'.

Drip. Drop_ Drop_ Drip.

Beside 'er chair is Jani, idly watchin' cool water trickle down the window from the back of a half-functionin' AC. Dust fuzz waves slowly, clingin' by grimy threads to the directional thingies of the AC. No wonder it's hot in here. I fan my shirt to cool myself. With his left hand curled into his body, while his right rests on the armchair, Jani sucks some of the drool from the corner of his mouth. Shit, I'd be tight as fuck if I couldn't walk around. Having to sit there awkwardly on his chair like dat must be horrible. No coochie, no chillin' with the homies. Shit devastatin'.

Drip. Drip. Drip. Drip.

To Ms. Jackson's notice, she quickly extends to clean 'im. She fails to reach and settles back into the chair as Jani moves his head away from 'er. He moves his eyes to the TV without movin' his head as saliva drip-dropped from the corner of his mouth and onto his chair, weirdly tho … at the same time as the AC water trickle. I sometimes wonder what's he thinkin' in there. Like … is he doin' dat on purpose? Because if he is, he must be dumb bored to be doin' dat, but I mean what else is he gon' do stuck in dat chair. I knew Marcus's cousin was … special needs, but man, it's always crazy to actually see it in person for this long. I wouldn't really pay much attention to 'im when I came over, not like he was really out like dat. He was usually just cooped in the room or just out with Ms. Jackson. In fact, I'd only really come thru when she wasn't here which was rare cuz Ms. Jackson never really left the surroundin' area of the projects. At most, she'd go as far as the park and das about it.

"So yeah … how old is Jani now?" I break the silence, pointin' at 'im while watchin' 'im drool.

Drip.

"My boy's twelve years old," she says with wide and slightly watery eyes.

Ms. Jackson, with one kid, was in 'er forties, but the weight and stress of it all made 'er look, well, more like a grandma than anythin' else. Shieet, she might as well be sixty with these damn plastic sofas. Who the fuck still has these? I lean into the armchair of the sofa makin' a huge suction sound. You can tell Ms. Jackson's one of those mothers dat be fienin' for they kids to stay young. Never lettin' 'em get older and always babyin' 'em into stayin'. With someone as crazy lookin' as her, they might just leave 'er. I'd definitely leave. Fuck, I'm trynna leave right now. Jani would too if he could walk. Lucky for her, this nigga ain't goin' nowhere. She continues, "He's growing so fast and I—"

"Hmm, he 'bout to be a grown ass man," I laugh awkwardly, as 'er eyes widen more than before showin' the reds on the top and bottom of 'er eye sockets. I realize my mistake. "My fault for cussin'."

"Oh, don't worry baby," she pauses, keepin' 'er eyes open for a lil. She blinks then opens 'em wide again—but not as wide where I could see the reds. She waves 'er right hand, unknowingly knockin' clothes from the small table to the left of 'er, "you just be a little careful how you speak about my boy."

I nod at her, showin' my bottom lip out in understandin'. I breathe in sharply, my shoulders in tension. She's wylin'. Bro … like … the minute Marcus said she was up here, I shoulda been done the math, like nah. I could've easily met up with 'im at the deli. Like … nah this lady givin' me weird vibes bro. Jani continues droolin' on his mode of transportation while lookin' intently at the turned off TV.

Drip. Drop_ Drip. Drip.

She looks to Jani, then back to me, and continues softenin' 'er face. "It's hard taking care of him sometimes, but y'know, a mother's love…"

"Yeah," I say dismissively as I look over to the dark hall. Marcus should've been out a minute ago. I knew I should've just waited at the deli or better yet, the crib. Maybe Marcus could've even talked a bit with daddy. It's been a minute. It would mean a lot to 'im too if he visited.

I look at Ms. Jackson, still talkin' about her son. She buggin' the fuck out. Smile. Smile. Nod your head so she thinks you listenin'. I breathe in sharply. Fuck, I shoulda stayed downstairs bro; I was just excited to see 'im after such a long time. My dumb ass … out here actin' like I wasn't gon' see 'im later anyways. This what I get for bein' a dick sucker. Marcus is a hard one to reach. Last time I saw 'im was two years ago, shortly after dat winter break link up, when comin' down from the Bronx back into Brooklyn. I stopped by his campus to chill for a bit. Then … nada. Like damn I know you busy up there.

When I saw 'im outside, I was excited. I was on my way to the bodega to meet up with 'im there, but I thought I might as well just come up, why not? Dat was clearly a mistake. I just thought he was gon' come up, get clothes, boom, then be out, but for some reason he ain't even let me into his room. I mean das always been Marcus, he's never liked people in his space like dat.

Now dat I think about it, even back then, he never let me into his room. We'd just chill in the park up the block or just play PS3 here in the livin' room. Once he moved here, he'd only let me come over when his aunt wasn't in the crib. I mean ... I can see why. Not dat this is my first time meetin' Ms. Jackson, but most def the first time havin' an extended conversation with 'er. This bitch crazy, respectfully.

"... *But* I love my son. When he was a baby—I prolly shouldn't say this," she chuckles deeply, "I used to play with the soft spots on his head."

"Hmm." I close my eyes as slow as I breathe. I can't believe this. I look over at Jani flailin' his curled arm against his chest. So, this why Jani retarded? Is that the right word I should use?

Drip. Drop_ Drop_ Drip.

"Ain't dat right, Jani?"

"*Ahhhh*," a cry comes from Jani as he struggles to pick his head up, his eyes still veerin' toward the TV. I breathe in long and sharp, openin' my eyes wide at 'im reachin' for the black rubber joystick in a flickin' fashion. I can't believe this shit. I can't believe *this* shit. I close my eyes and breathe out deeply as I bring my balled fist to my mouth.

I open my eyes and keepin' my face deadpan, while noddin', I muster one response, "Hmm."

"Are you tired baby? You seem tired," she says as she leans forward from 'er chair.

"No. Ms. Jackson, I—"

"*Wahhhhhh*"

A wild bawl comes down the hall. Ms. Jackson's face has no reaction like she ain't hear the cry. She stays there watchin' me as I look down the dark hall and back at 'er.

Drip. Drip. Drip. Drip.

"*Waaaaaaaaaaaaaaaahhhhhhhhhh*"

Ms. Jackson's eye twitches as she stares at me. She smiles and snaps out 'er trance and stands up. "Excuse me baby, das my other son, Daren. I'll be right back."

She leaves the room and shuffles down the hall whisperin' some shit about "damn baby always cryin'." I couldn't make it out. There was a slight silence cast in the room. Jani twisted his head back toward me and—

Drip.

Damn. How much saliva he got? Hydrated ass—

"*Waaaaaahhhhhh*"

I stand up from the sofa and look down the hall and then the door. Fuck he lookin' for in there—El Dorado? Buggin' out. I'on wanna be here with his crazy ass aunt. Bitch wild as fuck, I'm trynna dip. And brodie out here just salivatin' over his mode of transportation.

Drip. Drop_ Drip. Drip.

Got me on this uncomfortable ass ninety-nine cent store, plastic-covered sofa surrounded by laundry, actin' like all this shit on the floor smells like an angel's fart, some fuckin' water with a spritz of lemon and shit. I know this patterned sofa old as fuck too. Why the fuck it got the damn plastic on? You old bitch.

I take in a deep breath. Ight chill. Chill. Chill. It's not even dat serious. I'm just gon' head out and text Marcus I'm outside. It ain't even dat seri—

"*Wahhhhhh*"

Man dat baby needs to shut the fuck up. The clatterin' of slippers bible thumps heavily down the hallway as Ms. Jackson comes back, baby in arms. She sits back down and turns the now quiet teary-eyed baby over to face me, his face discombobulated with sleep lines. Chopped. These kids ugly as fuck. Goddamn. Sum 'bout the genes in Marcus's family ... it has to be. Wait. Whose baby is dat actually? How? Dat baby looks maybe like a bit more than a year old. Was she pregnant last time I heard? Nah. Also, ain't it hard to have kids after a certain age? And with who too? She fuckin' the neighbor?

The baby whimpers as he surveys the clothes-ridden livin' room. I smile at the ugly ass baby, wavin' at him. His wide eyes continue to scan the room, payin' me no attention. Ms. Jackson smiles at my gesture, her smile as wide as 'er eyes. She then looks down and slowly begins to caress the baby's head.

"So, what have you been doing lately, Jordan?" She asks while movin' some of the baby's hair to the side to reveal a small dent.

Makin' circular motions around the dent, she slowly presses the side of the baby's head.

I can't believe this. I look at the dent then back at 'er then back at the dent then back at 'er then back at the dent then back at 'er ... just to make sure she knows I know. And she does. I look at Jani, his watery eyes starin' at the baby. She continues to gently rub the outline of the pebble sized crater on the baby head.

Yeah nah, I'm out. I stand up slightly.

"Jordan?" she pushes 'er face forward, slightly tiltin' it to the side.

"Ms. Jackson, y'know, I was actually 'bout to head out." I smile forcefully.

"*Sit* back down," she says in a deep serious whisper. Her lip quivers in anger as 'er eyes widen more to show the reds again. She catches herself and puts on the face she had before, smiles a little, and with a sultry, deeper voice says, "It's rude to leave in the middle of a conversation."

I look at the dark hallways. My body grows heavier on the couch, sinkin' deeper into the plastic. I look at Jani starin' back with red eyes, shiftin' his gaze from me to the TV to the baby. She nods 'er head continuously almost like as if I were talkin', waitin' for me to say sum. Fuck.

"What are you up to lately?" She asks.

"I— s—school, and work."

DRIP. DROP. DROP. DRIP.

"Where you go to school again baby?"

"Uh ... Brook—" I clear my throat and look at Jani with his head down, grimly lookin' at the baby and then at me, "Brooklyn College."

"Oh. Are you on dat lil scholarship thang?" She dips 'er finger further into the baby head, scoopin' round the edges like she diggin' into chocolate puddin'. "Susior. Sesior—"

"Excelsior." I swallow slightly and awkwardly.

"Oh yes."

...

She nods at me as she continues to swirl 'er finger inside the baby's head like you trynna get the last bits of chocolate out the puddin' cup.

...

"Ms. Jackson?"

"Yes."

"Ms. Jackson, it's none of my business but—"

"Yo," Marcus comes out the dark hallway, bag slung over his shoulder, "we out?"

Blop—I spring up as the plastic suctions off my ass. I look back to see a deep crater where I was sittin'. Yo ... if I had stayed any longer in dat seat, I would've melted into it. I swiftly walk toward the door, pushin' Marcus to the side as I go outside into the hallway. Thank God.

I look back at Ms. Jackson now caressin' the baby's hair forward, hidin' the dip on his head. Get me out of here. She's tweakin' bro. I look at Jani lookin' at the baby and then the

TV and then at me, his eyes red and wellin'. Damn son, dat shit's tough. Should I say sum? It must be frustratin' bein' in dat chair son. Especially with your mom bein' this fuckin' crazy. We gotta call CPS on this bitch or sum. Nah ... I'on even know what the fuck goin' on here.

DRIP. DRIP. DRIP. DRIP.

"Bye Jordan." She looks at me eyes wide and then turns to Marcus with a deeper voice, "Marcus, come visit me more often. Oh, and did you get my present? I mai—"

"Yeah," he says blandly as he turns the knob of the door and opens it. I turn around and as Marcus closes the door, Ms. Jackson waves slowly till its shut.

DRIP.

"Bro, you dead took ya sweet time!"

We walk down the dimly lit corridor, around to the elevator door. Marcus presses the down button.

"What are you talking about? We were in there for like," he flips his wrist to look at his watch, "eight minutes."

"Nah, never again. Your auntie tweakin'."

"What?"

"Yo. She was in there rubbin' dat lil nigga head bro," the elevator doors open, and we walk in, "and she just mad weird ... like ... Fuck's wrong with 'er?"

"Man..." he presses the first floor button and shakes his head, a wild expression of 'where do I even begin?' washes his face, "she's always been that weird and creepy. That's why I was always at yours. At least you ain't have to live with her."

"Yeah," I sigh deeply. "Bro. Dat young'un gon' end up fucked up like ya cousin Jani if she keep dippin' into dat baby head like puddin'."

"That's insensitive. You know he has a genetic condition." He sucks his teeth and looks at me sideways. "Plus massaging a baby's head like that won't do anything like that."

The elevator door closes.

I wave my hand ina scoopin' motion. "Bro, she was in there diggin' dat shit in. He gon' come up ... retarded."

"It doesn't work—man, I don't think we supposed to be saying that word."

"Nigga, this ain't academia," I suck my teeth, "y'all be more preoccupied on sayin' the right things than doin' the right things. You ain't never told 'er to stop doin' dat? Call CPS or some shit?"

"Call the authorities?" he questions. "You? I never thought I'd see the day."

"I mean, then who?" I say back.

"She's a decent mom. She's weird, yeah, but it's inconsequential," he huffs out, blowin' out air sharply from his nose as he chuckles slightly. He disappointingly smirks and shakes his head as he says, "Man…"

Fuck you shakin' your head for like I said sum stupid? If anyone needs to be disappointed, it's me. I was in dat hoe creeped the fuck out. Just for you to get whatever the fuck it is you got in your bag, which brings me to the question, "You got what you needed?"

"Yeah." Marcus looks down to the muck-covered floor and sniffs, strappin' the other flap of his bag on his shoulder. Lookin' up and straight at the muddied reflection of himself on the dirty metal door of the elevator, he joins both the bag flaps from opposite sides together. He breathes in and out almost like a sigh, "Yeah."

CHAPTER 2

FLACO, RAULI, AND PUERCO

ABEL
[Barbershop]
[The Bronx]
[10:03 a.m.]

"I'm next." I look up from my phone and sit in Flaco's chair in front of three more waitin' customers. See, y'all be scared to say you're up next. I'm not. Then again, those three weren't waitin' for this barber.

Y'see ... A man's barber is a man's brother. The fate of a hairline lies within those capable of joinin' the hand and the blade, and those who can make *that blade*, an extension of their vision. Dat's right. Reader, a man's barber must be visionary to lay eyes on the most chopped mammoth lookin' muhfucka and turn 'im into *the* coochie drippin' *king* dat he knows he is. Unfortunately, my barber is capable of no such thing. Well ... at least this one isn't. I know it's against code to switch up on your barber like dat, *but* if you're loyal to all three of 'em, and they don't know about each other, then what's the harm? Right out of the Bronx Dominican fuckboy handbook. And they say we don't know about commitment to one thing. I'm committed to all three. Yesssir.

Flaco shakes the cape on the chair as I walk over and sit in it. "Lesgo."

"Yo, forreal, do my drop fade right this time," I gotta let 'im know cuz last time he had one side lighter than the other, "I got work tonight AND I'm trynna meet up with my peoples later."

The deep moans of the clipper graze the side of my head—my ears folded against itself by my on-and-off longtime barber, Flaco. Flaco has been cuttin' my hair for years, but his skills, as opposed to improvin', had only worsened. Flaco was, as his affectionately given nickname could tell, a typical skinny Dominican. Y'know the type: lightskin to medium brown depending on the season, bird chest, three kids, an unfulfilled dream of opening up his own barbershop ... *that* nigga. He's been whisperin' dat dumb shit into my ears—pause—since I was seven years old: "No te apure papi, que cuando yo tenga lo mio, to' grati pa ti." Since then, not once has he left this chair, nor have I received a free cut.

"No, no, no, I gatchu, papi. I gif you wat you want dis time." Flaco licks his lips, steps back, and sways his long centipede body from side to side looking at what's to be worked with; the misfortune I'll have to call a hairline.

"Pause," I chuckle.

Flaco puts down the clippers and shuffles his messy station around lookin' for a different guard. His station, over the years, stayed consistently messy. Y'know the vibes ... The two big Brugal bottles where he drops his used razors have been on its brim for a minute, as long as I can even remember, a testament to the many years he had been working under someone else, never improvin', never pursuin' his dreams. Surroundin' the bottles were, what I think are his actual clippers set and sprays and shit, but I wouldn't know cuz I never see 'em. Bunch of paper littered his station like a thirteen-year-old dat just discovered the fine art of beatin' his shmeat. Oh, the good ole' days. He swats the papers away, some landing at the edge of the station, and some off to their doom, where they'd contrast with the hair-covered floor … forever. Well, until they get swept.

He picks up and puts the guard on the clippers. "Que pause ni que pause, I can't pause deh movie."

"Nah dat whole statement … man … never mind."

Flaco nears the groanin' clippers to my ears before stoppin', turning off the clippers, and looking up mesmerized—his undivided attention given to the contents on the TV.

"Flaco?" I say.

He stays lookin'. A couple laughs come from the back of the barbershop, their eyes also stuck to the TV. The barbershop was quieter than usual. On regular days, music would blare so loudly, so profoundly, dat it could greet you and shake your hand from down the block … but not today. Today the crowd was mostly quiet, which is unknown for this specific species in their natural habitat.

Y'see, Dominicans are always loud, but especially in a barbershop. A bunch of 'em hicks from the campo, they never got past havin' to shout at one another in the mountains—hence the loud music and shoutin', now as normalized as the physical brawls in a NYC love story. In fact, barbershops are the loudest thangs in the Boogie Down Bronx, right after the revvin' sounds of motorbikes at 2 a.m. and the gunshots and sirens dat follow it.

But today is different. A movie was playing in the shop, a must-see. I mean it has to be cuz what other reason is there for 'em to be *this* quiet, *this* early, watchin' *this* movie. This type of silence doesn't even happen durin' baseball season. No music, no game analysis, no shoutin', no married men bitchin' 'bout the lack of hookah and bitches—a glizzy fest—at last night's party. Nun of dat. Just silence. Just extreme focus on the TV, which is as committed as I'd ever seen a group of platanos be to something other than hatin' and cheatin'. Even the customers on the chairs are viewin' the movie with their undivided attention, and from their age, you could assume half of 'em are crack babies.

"Flaco?"

He ignores me again. I swing around my chair like a four-hundred-dollar bundle to get a better look at the TV. I look at the TV—looming over our heads in the corner like the amount of gamblin' debt and infidelities each barber has—and smirk, huffin' some air out, as it turns into a chuckle, "I can't believe this."

I dead can't believe it. I shake my head slowly as it takes me but a few seconds to realize what I was disappointingly watchin'. Two actors twirl about on a green backdrop, punching and kickin'. One of the actors, a woman, pushes the man away. Now from a distance, both extendin' their vibrating arms toward one another, they scream. She shouts, "I will liberate," while black wires pull the man away into the corner, keeping him from what I'm assuming is goin' to be a real shitty ass CGI blast. Zooming in and out of focus, the camera follows the man with a green bodysuit catchin' the flyin' man attached to the wires, now quivering in defeat as his catcher waves into the camera. The ghetto.

A unifyin' howl fills the room dissipatin' the bit of silence the barbershop would ever know in its existence. The barbers all high-five and dap one another as the customers, unanimously, sit there unamused, suckin' their teeth at the results of the battle.

"Uno ni la tiene que ver ahora en noviembre," says one of the barbers.

"Yo, eta pelicula va ta heavy' con esa baina qu'ello le ponen, Siiiii," Flaco whispers in my ear.

I scuff 'im off my ear and continue to watch the blonde woman stand triumphantly, swayin 'er hair in an epic hero shot. Huh ... bitch looks familiar. Ain't this the sequel to dat movie dat got mad backlash two years ago? I squint my eyes a bit. Yeah ... it is. Hollywood must be starvin' if they made another one. *The Liberator: Growing Knee Pain*. I can't wait for the controversy this movie gon' cause when it comes out. But fuck allat, how are we even watchin' this? This supposed to come out in November.

I see all the barbers dappin' and dickridin' Rauli. Ahh, dat makes sense. This man Rauli got dat shit three months in advance ... before release, before the CGI edits. Of course it'd be Rauli, what other man in this place got pull like Rauli ... no one. I watch as the TV screen fades to black as the recordin' shows a man puttin' his phone in his pocket. Wow ... bottom of the barrel. Dat's wild. What the fuck is this? Man, there's so much to unpack here. Like ... I deadass don't understand how he has dat much pull like ... I mean, this the man who got the fuckin ... uh ... the fuckin laundromat machines across the street for free, and they do *not* play with their money.

"Flaco, where you goin'?" I look at Flaco gettin' ready to go dap Rauli on the other side of the barber shop.

"Pero que lo tuyo, Abel," he reacts and scrunches his face like he done smelled his shit breath sitting on his upper lip. He brushes the guard of the clippers aggressively. "Reelah."

He better start brushin' his teeth dat aggressively if he gon' be talkin' to me like dat.

"Que tengo planes Flaco, lezgoooo." I clap my hands, one-two, to hurry 'im up. "I got plans. People waitin' for me ... I got a show tonight too. You know dat."

He picks up the clippers again, fondlin' his messy station around lookin' for sum. I take my phone out my pocket to see the time: 10:13 a.m. Damn. He better do this shit quick. I check my text messages: two from Alex, sum, sum, project, food—she better be talkin' 'bout food— ha-ha, One from Jordan, not openin' dat ... aaannndddd ... none from Marcus. Fuckin' clown, I'm the reason you even coming anyways. You could at least hit your boy up.

"Easy my friend, easy—" Flaco says condescendingly, swayin' his hands and head singy-songy like he calmin' some fuzzy baby. He's had a lot of practice doin' dat considerin' his three kids—who am I kiddin, he prolly ain't seen 'em kids dat often when little. Oh reader, have I yet mentioned dat Flaco is trash at his job and as a father? Oh ... I have. Oh. About the job, but not the father bit. Well, let me continue.

"You know dat." I sigh deeply as Flaco continues to work, foldin' my ear down again while the gripin' clippers go to work.

Damn. I breathe in deeply and out as Flaco begins the haircut.

It's been a minute since I'd seen the boys ... plus Alex. Pat on the back for being inclusive, especially when dat inclusivity come from 'round these parts. Y'know ... I'm 'bout to say sum the Bronx in me wouldn't say out loud ... I miss 'er sometimes. I used to see 'er on campus all the time walkin' with the Beckies from upstate and Cali, all tokenized and shit, talkin' some dumb shit 'bout the patriarchy. Funny dat they'd go to parties and have those same friends of hers get they back blown out by, yeah, you guessed it reader, the patriarchy. Talk about being in bed with the enemy.

I miss makin' fun of 'er tho. I think dat's what it is ... I feel no greater satisfaction knowin' my time on earth is bein' well spent angerin' Alex. Ionno what it is about it dat just makes it so enjoyable. Maybe, it's cuz I never had a younger sister or brother to bother in my infancy, someone for me to see suffer as I let go of all the stress and bullshit I had to deal with. Lookin' back, Alex did just fine.

I met 'er freshman year in high school debate club. Before dat, I was lost, emotionally unavailable, deeply troubled ... and ... pfffttt ha-ha I'm just fuckin witchu. Where was I? Oh yeah, I met 'er in debate club and I was lookin' to start trouble. In fact, I joined cuz of her. She used to be a "free the nipple" type of feminist activist. Y'know, the ones dat detract from every social movement by doing incredibly shitty or unimportant and controversial takes. Dat one. And those are the easiest people to bother. In club meetings, I'd purposely position myself as a contrarian, and most times, I ain't even believe in the shit I was arguin'. I should say dat, reader, before you go and cancel my creator for making a nuanced character. Anyways, she'd be mad tight for no reason too, like c'mon beloved ... it's just human rights. I used to envy her tho, for carin' so much about these things. I never could. Seemed to me, at the time, there was more happening around here to even be thinking about drone missiles falling on poor children in the Middle East. But hey, at least a woman is sendin' those missiles, so I guess we a rather progressive imperialist state. But forreal though, she hated me for no reason. She made me sit in the back of the bus every time we went to conventions, like Rosa ain't fight for my rights too, bitch. One particular convention in sophomore year, we had to debate in pairs. Alex and I ended up formulating arguments and debating against what she claimed to be "bigots." Me, personally, I just think they hated poor, low-income people, which is fair ... I do teeter on the line of hatin' my circumstances and hatin' myself. It's a delicate balance.

Anyways, we won, of course, I mean, c'mon reader, you see how witty I am. How could I ever lose? She was mesmerized at my brilliance, shocked at my nuance, engrossed in my knowledge, and I was deep in 'er kewchay—or so I thought I'd be. But no, I ain't receive shit for my intellect because it was then she finally got it. She finally understood dat I was mostly fucking around in the debate club. It was a way to beef up my extracurricular and to stay out the streets.

Through the club meetings, dat event, our mutual friendships with Marcus and Jordan, me and 'er stayed friends throughout high school. As I matured alongside Alex, I found new ways to anger her, strengthening our friendship. By the end of senior year, we were both excited to go to college together and—thanks to me, a man—she, a woman, became a critical thinker. Not to man-credit steal, or whatever fancy, academic word there is for the term. There's prolly a word for it. Shit, I'll take credit for dat too. I miss her ... makin' fun of 'er ... I mean.

Jordan ... I'on miss so much. Y'know how in a group, there's always those two people dat are just friends because everyone else is friends? Dat's us. I'on give a fuck 'bout 'im. Y'know what ... deadass ... I can do more time without seein' his ugly ass up over here. Always 'round 'ere anyways brazenly nutting in these dusty ass hoes. Like deadass … go get tested. Again, the ghetto.

But if I really miss anyone, it's Marcus—no homo tho. Bougie ass Ivy League nigga think he better than us. I mean he's better than Alex and Jordan, but c'mon now … after all those years he borrowed *my* history homework, you'd think he'd come up here and express gratitude for helpin' 'im get in. Kiss my feet—pause—no foot fetish. His ugly ass right there too, he could just take the train uptown to El Bronx … shittin' me. I ain't seen his weak ass hairline in a while, and he knows time moves differently when you're a degenerate, so it's been more than just a *minute*.

I watch as Flaco continues along the back and then to the other side, carvin' out the bald line.

… Ay … yo …

Who the fuck taught 'im to cut hair? I cheat—I mean … I *explore* my options outside of Flaco, go to different barbers, and come back to 'im—pause—and now he knows how to please me? Big pause. Damn … I might have to tip 'im today. Pause again. Fuck. I really hope he fucks it up—pause—slightly to where it's fine, but I'on got to tip 'im. Pause.

The barbershop door swings opens. A chubby figure dat needs nearly the entire door open comes in, "Puerco," Flaco's oldest son. No, his name is not *puerco*, like pig. Who the fuck gon' name they kid pig? Dat's his nickname.

Yes, his nickname's pig cuz he's a fat, dirty fuck. Or so they say … Ionno … I'on spend time wit'im to know. He's also Flaco's son, so on top of havin' his own struggles, he gotta carry his pops' as well. His bestowed moniker replaced his name years ago to the point where … if I'm bein honest … I'on even know this kid's name like dat. Prolly some wild Dominican ass name trynna be American like Jason—but said as Jah-son. Or some name fuckery such as Stanly, but spelled Estanli. Whatever shitty, creative name it is … it don't matter. His name is Puerco. Shit's kinda sad tho cuz the barbers treat 'im like shit, which is fair, but sometimes they take it too far, and just violate the kid for no reason. Flaco bein' the fat juicy pussy dat he is—pause—just laughs with the other barbers instead of defendin' his own kid. Kids only fifteen and already havin' body image issues cuz of these ugly, fat ass, light skin "me no black, papi" ass niggas. And y'know what … as he should. It's the right of passage dat we all went through and, in some ways, it toughens you. It's a toxic tradition dat propels forth this cycle of violence and abuse and I hope it never dies out. There's sarcasm in there. Reader, y'know it's hard sometimes to put it into word format, but just take everything I say with a grain of salt.

Flaco stops cuttin' my hair, turnin' to face his son. "Mijo, coge la e'coba ahi y barreme, por favor."

The kid picks up the broom and starts sweepin' the surrounding area as Flaco continues, my hair fallin' to the ground meetin' the dirty bristles of the broom.

"Miralo ahiiiiiiii," a barber sings, "Puerco, ven pa'ca … barreme aqui tambien."

Puerco's face freezes at being asked to approach the barbers in the back. He walks over there slowly and stops, slightly hesitant at the idea of bein' close to any of 'em. There was this one time where they made 'im get on the scale dat's in the bathroom to see how fat he was. Which doesn't sound dat bad, but when you're thirteen, dat shit is everythin'. You're a developin' kid in the world. Prolly thinkin' 'bout some pussy and sports and shit. It's kinda cruel. I mean don't get me wrong, I laughed … Not even gon' hold you, shit was kinda funny, but I'm a better man now than I was two years ago. I look at Flaco's reflection and see his bird chest tense up, his eyes showcasin' his racin' thoughts, pondering as to whether he should say sum. I'on know why he stressin'. He ain't gon' do shit. He might as well not waste time and continue focusing on cuttin' my hair.

Puerco gets close and sweeps the hair on the floor near their station. The nearby barbers, except Rauli, poke and pinch at his fat. Rauli shakes his head, in disapproval, but keeps cuttin' hair without ever saying anythin'. It be like dat tho.

"Oye pero le ta dando al gym," one of the barbers says, grabbin' Puerco' shirt and lifting it up.

The other barbers stop cuttin' hair and go see Puerco's belly and laughs at his stretch marks and excess skin, the product of bullying and the dedication dat followed it. Important lesson to those dat say bullying is wrong. Puerco was slimmer this summer than the one before. He prolly hittin' the gym since everybody in here bullies 'im about his weight. It's not like these muhfucka's the perfect image of health and fitness either. They all got beer bellies, and fried neurons and shit, but it's typical old head Dominican shit. Out here "hablando mierda" talkin' shit, 'bout everybody even when they themselves don't got it either. I remember when they used to do dat shit to me. Those were sad years.

Man ... I should say sum. Nah. Am I really the type who would deprive a man of character development? But also, am I the type of person who would just let this go by me? Yes, I am. Oh ... don't judge me reader ... I'm a proud piece of shit. I'on give a fuck what you think 'bout me. I would definitely let 'em fat-shame 'im, *but* makin' fun of people in defense of others might seem noble, so why not?

"Dejen a ese muchacho tranquilo," I say in his defense, "Sancocho, tu ere el modelo d'el ... hablando mierda como si tu no ta ma pesao qu'el, a quien tu cree que a el le ta copiando, e a ti."

The barbers erupt in laughter. Reader, this is America, learn Spanish. You'd prolly understand if you paid attention, but I know you just google translated your way through Spanish class, so do the same here. Some of the customers sittin' in the chair laugh as the others awkwardly chuckle. The comedian in me searchin' for a bigger laugh continues.

"U'tede hablando mierda como si uno no aprende la cosa mala e de u'tede," I continue, as Gordo lets go of Puerco, "oye se llama puerco, pero no te lo coma, Sancocho."

Rauli chuckles and winks at me, no homo.

"Dejenlo tranquilo, que por lo meno ta ahi en el gym," I comment as they accept defeat, cowardly goin back to cuttin' hair, hidin' their reaction to their painful truths through their fake smiles, laughs, and the nonchalant *chuipi*.

Lookin' back, all the shit talk relatives and the barbers did was necessary to givin' me the quick tongue to disrespect the shit out these grown-ups. Dominicans will take your physical defects and make it your nickname. My moniker ... well I had several. *Hach'e diente*. Big teeth. *Haitiano*, which is just plain out colorist, but what can you expect from people whose entire culture revolves around self-hate. I mean ... the DR is what happens when you let a bunch of house niggas start a country. But the one dat hurt me the most ... *huevin*. Lil dick. Oh, how dare they talk about my manhood. Oh ... the pains I had to endure as a boy. Woe is me and all dat shit. But now I'm a man, and unbeknownst to 'em all—but not their daughters—I pack heavy. Heavy like the tanks these mutual dick riders send back home filled with miscellaneous shits to their mothers, their twisted way of lovin' cuz if they really wanted to, they'd just bring 'er here to the States. I guess they never forgave or got past the *chancletazos* and belt-whoopings, the discipline they still so desperately need.

Lookin' back, the struggle is cruel when you growing up in the city, but especially here in the Bronx. It leaves you scarred and in constant need to assert yourself in a world dat was never meant for you, and the worst part is bein' cognizant of dat. Dat's why the more you toughen up, the better life gets. You think I'mma take lip from niggas dat barely finished middle school, maybe high school, in a third world country? Fuck outta here. There ain't shit anyone can say to me anymore.

Puerco walks back and picks up the broom, givin' me a smile. You welcome kid. He goes back to sweepin' the floor, gatherin' the fallin' hair from my head into a nice lil pile, which he scoops into the garbage. He leans the broom on the wall and comes closer to Flaco's station. He signals Flaco to get closer, whisperin' sum in his ear, sum to which Flaco just nods with an indifferent face.

"Yo, thank you man," he says, "I appreciate it."

"Stay in the gym and keep hustlin bro," I fan my arm out of the cape and extend my fist to 'im, "don't let 'em get you like dat."

"Yeah," he meets his fist to mine.

Flaco twirls me in the chair to face the transparent front of the shop. It's a good day today. Sunny and hot, but not hot enough where you're sticky type of hot. Just enough where the booty shorts come out ... not dat it takes much for 'em to come out anyways. I watch the people walk by in the streets. The mothers with trailin' kids, the shirtless rebels in bikes, the cars blarin' music, the kids excited at the sound of the ice cream truck miles away before even parents could hear. It all paints a weird picture to me, all of it imbued with the summer feel of 2006 or some deeply lost memory. Amongst the multitude of people in the street, one thing catches more eyes than anythin' else: From the corner, crossin' the street, a shorty with the fatty walks toward the laundromat—her laundry bag over her shoulder, sitting on and supported by 'er ass more than 'er arms. Shit dummy fat. Wild fat. She looks familiar, but then again she might just have dat look to 'er. If you spend enough time on IG, you'd know it when you see it. It's dat one look every woman but Black women are copyin'. This bitch tho is definitely an originator. Flaco peeps the booty as she turns to enter the laundromat and drops 'er big ass bag of clothin' and says, "Esa morena tiene. Mirale la nargota a esa."

"Esa no tiene na," I say about the big booty shorty.

"Dique que no tiene," Flaco says with no shame. In perfect English, "That's a fat ass."

And indeed it is. Shit so fat he said dat shit in English perfectly, no Spanish accent or nothin'. I watch as she enters the laundromat, all eyes greetin' 'er. She drops the bag off to the owner with a smile, passin' some money to 'im. He nods and waves 'er goodbye as she leaves the laundromat as fast as she entered it. The owner leans over and around to the door and sees dat she makes it safely to the end of the street and around the corner. Aww, what a nice man. I bet he takes care of all his customers like dat. The shorties with ass and nothin' more to offer. Sounds like sum Jordan would be into. Dat would be his type. Shit who knows dat might just be shorty he come through to drop dick for. He couldn't possibly entertain' anythin' more. He ain't got enough brain to get 'im a booty with a brain, but a booty without one is def within reach.

"Ass is not the only thing you need in a good woman," I clarify what I meant.

"Yeah okay," he says dismissively.

Of course, Flaco wouldn't know about a woman past 'er body. How could he? How do you look at Flaco and decide you'd want to have kids with 'im. She clearly has to be all body and no brain, and thinkin' about how fat Puerco is … she definitely got a lot of it. Me personally, my brain … I can't wrap dat shit around it. Shit just blows mine. Dat makes absolutely no sense to me, but I guess dat's the love shit people be talkin' 'bout. Or maybe it's just desperation. Loneliness could make anyone crazy … but crazy enough to marry Flaco? Nah. Mental illness the only answer.

Flaco twirls me around to face the mirror to see his work. Fuck. I might have to tip 'im today—pause. I turn my head to the sides lookin' at any defect my hair may have, but no. He throws the clipper down on his workstation and picks up a razor edge to finish off the line up. He goes 'round meticulously.

Flaco swings over to the back of my head workin' the back scrapin' the last bit of hair with the razor edge. He brushes off my neck, grabs the blower, blowing all the hairs from my face. He grabs the cape and shakes it in the air, as hair falls to the ground. I stand from the chair and look up into the mirror. Damn. He blended the lines well on my fade. He ain't fuck up my waves. The lines are crisp. It's not bad. Fuck. I guess this is it. He finally did it. I'm proud of 'im. I ain't gon' tell 'im dat tho, but man, it only took 'im a couple dozen tries over the years, but finally. I look good as hell … maybe Mami will finally see how well I'm refinin' the race.

I open up my wallet and pull out thirty dollars. I give it to 'im as he wears a face of surprise.

"Keep it all."

CHAPTER 3

A BUTTER ROLL

MARCUS
[Neighborhood Projects]
[Brooklyn]
[9:58 a.m.]

We walk out the elevator, around the corner, and past the wire mesh glass wall with a single metal door. We pressed through to be surrounded by the all-familiar, tall, identical towers that sequestered the area in its own pocket. Back in the thirties and forties, this was where "they" stuffed hundreds of thousands of "undesirables" in corners of the boroughs. You have the supermarket and the bodegas in the corners, the laundry in the basement of each building, the public schools up the block—underfunded and overcrowded. You have everything you could ever need around you if you never realized how it was all designed to keep you there. These were projects, and they all facilitated conformity. Regardless of whether the reason was to keep you down or to keep you out of sight, I had to leave it.

The bums who once stood around here when I was a little kid have all died and been replaced with the new state of the art institutionalized bodies, pipelined to work for someone else, whether that be at or below a minimum wage or with prison labor when the NYPD needs their monthly quotas. The education system failed them, and living comfortably in their mediocrity, with neither connections nor resources, was never an option. Those who don't have are not allowed to be comfortable and mediocre, so when I got that acceptance letter, I never looked back. I got into Columbia and dormed there. I came back to get clothes or stuff I needed ever so often, but I never stayed for long. Coming back evoked an ambivalent feeling, a sense of nostalgia and sadness knowing that I'll never be the same kid walking through these same streets in the same way. Still all the same, I was glad to leave it … at the end of the day, I could always come back to it. It will always be here. After all, it never changes.

Pulling on the straps of my backpack, Jordan and I walk toward the corner bodega. Nothing about the street had changed since I was gone. In fact, in an ever-changing city, this has never changed. Three bums with nothing to do in front of the bodega—check. The streets filled with shattered glass from henny and beer bottles, mixed with cigarette butts and crushed leaves—check. The constant swamp ass smell of the homeless lingering in the air from 'round the corner … is new, but a bad change here is really no change at all. Bad things happening here is a constant. Some things, while the small details may differ, never change no matter how much time we give it.

"Yo 'member we gotta meet up with Alex and Abel later," Jordan reminds me as he types into his phone, "gon' send a text in the group chat."

"Yeah."

We walk down the block, crossing the street onto the opposite side. I stand outside the sticker-ridden bodega front, pause to admire it ... it hasn't changed. I walk through the door and greet the owner behind the bulletproof counter.

"Yo what's good Ock?" Jordan knocks on the countertop, eyeing the swishers, condoms, and telephone cards in the back.

"Hey," the owner looks up, pauses, then smiles in realization, "oh, it's you. Where you been, my fr'end? How are you?"

"All good, all good. Just school." I laugh and look toward the back of the bodega, past the chip stands. "Is Papi here?"

"Pause," Jordan chimes.

"Yeah, he's in the back, but he'll be at the grill in a minute."

I walk toward the grill and wait. I look back to the front of the bodega, Jordan scanning the chip stand, visibly distraught by it all. He stands there in silence for a bit, presses his lips against his teeth, and goes up to the owner. "So Ock, you gon' disrespect me with these prices again?"

"My fr'end, everything keeps rising, rent, tax, bills, and everything."

"Yeah ... I know." Jordan looks pensively, picks up a bag of chips, and waves it at me. "Bro ... a dollar for this bum ass bag?"

Damn. Only a couple years ago, we could've bought that same "bum ass bag" for twenty-five cents. Actually, that's almost a decade ago really. Time does move fast.

Jordan and the owner continue to talk about "hood economics" and the competition. Apparently, a new café had opened up down the block a few months ago. A lot of the new people that had moved into the adjacent neighborhood and would come into the bodega, are now frequenting the café.

Competition. Jordan begged the question: how do bodegas survive when there's so many of them around? Even before the café, there's a bodega on every block, sometimes even two, corner to corner ... yet they've always shown no signs of struggle over the years.

"Y'all dead pushin' weight," Jordan jokes, "shit's actually OD how y'all..."

"*Ooohhh shitt,*" a loud scream comes from the back and into the grilling area, "look who's back."

"Dimelo, Papi," I turn around and greet pops.

"Pause," Jordan screams from the front.

"Shut up, Jordan." Pops's face turns serious, then light, pointing at Jordan. He says to me, "So you still hanging out with *ete come-mierda?*"

Pops always had a way in asking rhetoricals. Jordan was always talking shit as a kid, hence his anointed nickname, *come-mierda*—shit-eater. You spew what you eat, I guess. Ironic since this bodega technically fed us. Pops, Ock, and us, we go way back. Jordan and I had been coming into the bodega ever since we could remember. Whether that be with Jordan's dad—Dillion—or mine. We'd come here after school and get snacks, talk with Ock and Pops, eat our snacks at the park, then rush back to Jordan's to eat actual food. We were growing boys—a vacuum that consumed from the pockets of others and our own—and when everything went dry, Pops would cover us. From time to time, Pops would give us a chopped cheese and let us split it in half. For our birthdays, he would give us each our own. He cared for us like that.

"Y'know how it is Pops, he's a clown, but you can't choose family." I watch as Jordan grabs a packet of Sour Power straws and slaps it on the counter. I shake my head. "You can't choose family."

"Yeah, but you can choose when to come back," he snaps. "You go up to that big school and don't wanna come back, huh? You busy with the girls up there or what?"

"Nah, just school and work."

"Damn, so no girls?" He smirks. "That hurts me even more."

"More than work?"

"Well, we don't work 24/7/365, so I'mma take full offense when you don't come visit for that." He starts laughing and smiling. "Now women are 24/7/365. They take time and dedication."

"Yeah." I scratch the back of my head and step back.

"It's been what—"

"Two years or something like that." After graduating high school and going off to college, I came back to visit for Christmas during my freshman year.

"I think I saw you walkin' around like two months ago." He shoots straight.

"Y—yeah, I probably—uh—came real quick ... y'know ... to get some shorts."

"You should've stopped by. Come visit more man," Pops says earnestly. He sees my face, changes his tone, and turns toward the grill. "So whatchu want?"

He always joked about it—that I would get enamored with being up there and that I'd never come back. I always told him it wouldn't be as such, but he was right. I had forgotten about them and moved to bigger heights. I know it's wrong, but I can't help feeling like there's nothing here for me anyways. The only way is up and forward from here. I didn't know it then, but that Christmas was my last time really coming back for a long time. Yeah, I came for clothes, but I never really came back, never checked in, nor visited folks from around. Pops probably understands that I'm just busy

A BUTTER ROLL · 47

and I'm trying to move past it all. He probably understands that coming back just became like taking a step back. He understands. He just wishes it were different. It just feels like there's nothing here for me—

"Lemme get dat beggeneggencheeee, Pops," Jordan interjects, swinging his arm around me as I look up at the menu. I scuff him off me. It's too hot for that. He looks up to the prices on the sign and continues, "Damn. Shit's dead four bucks now? Nah lemme get a BLT, then. Das three fif. All these prices goi—"

"And you Marcus?"

What would I want? Should I just get a bacon egg and cheese or—I look at Jordan, then back to the menu, then over at Pops already getting started on Jordan's sandwich, and smile softly. It's just like back then. I look up at the menu again and say, "Can I get a butter roll?"

Jordan looks at me dumbfounded, scrunching his face as he usually does when someone says something wildly out of place. Pops turns around and laughs as he begins to cut a bread roll in half.

"Nigga said butter roll. My son reminiscin'. I ain't had dat shit in years." Jordan shook his head as he walked further into the bodega to the fridges in the back, taking out two Arizona bottles—one watermelon, the other iced tea. He comes back and hands one to me, slapping my chest with the back of his hand and pointing at the menu. "Bro, I got you. Order *anything* you want."

"Nah, I really want a butter roll though."

"Shiieett, give him what he wants Pops," he says, opening up his Arizona bottle and taking a swig. "No homo tho."

The butter roll was the go-to when we were broke kids. They were less than a dollar at the time and, though they held no nutritional value, those rolls held hunger at arm's length till we got actual food. Some days the chopped cheese, the bacon egg and cheese, the BLT, they would all taste different—but a butter roll was consistent. It never disappointed, and how could it. It's melted butter on a roll ... it was the bare minimum.

Pops prepares the sandwich slowly to keep us here longer. He knows it will be a while till he sees us again, so he's probably savoring the moment.

"So Marcus, you still studying uhhh ... ?"

"I'm double majoring now ... business and economics."

"You've always been a smart kid." Pops's eyes widen. He sighs, as he flips the bacon and scrambled eggs. "Don't lose sight of what's important."

"Be careful pops," Jordan chimes, "nothing more important than chasin' a bag to 'im."

"What you trynna do when you graduate?" Pops ignores Jordan.

"I'm not sure to be honest." I had interned in corporate jobs, start-ups, different companies, but none of it really stuck with me. I could probably go back to any of those places I interned, get a full-time job, but none of it felt fulfilling then so why would it now. It all felt surgical, just a job managing accounts, shaking hands, faking enthusiasm, and getting paid.

"Well, whatever you do..." Pops was wrapping up Jordan's bacon egg and cheese at this point and setting it on top of my easily prepared butter roll, "...don't be a stranger to us. Come visit."

"Yeah," I say hesitantly so as not to make it sound like a promise.

Jordan takes the sandwiches and walks to the front and sets them on the counter next to the Sour Power straws and his Arizona. He begins to talk to Ock and points at me, or more likely the Arizona, as he takes out his wallet.

I look back at Pops. "See you later."

"I hope so man."

"It's cool Pops," Jordan chimes again, "I'll be back in a few."

Pops just shakes his head and goes back to his grill, a long face on him. He swings a towel over his shoulder and starts to clean the area on the grill he had made our sandwich on.

I walk up to the front and see the sandwiches bagged, each separately. "Nah, put them both in the same bag."

"Ew, why you want our sandwiches to touch?"

"It's a waste of a bag man." I put my sandwich and Arizona in his bag and gave the other back to Ock, who gladly took it.

"This nigga care about the environment." Jordan shakes his head laughing, swigging his drink.

"Man, shut up." I grab the black bag and straddle my backpack, grabbing both sides of the straps and anchoring them further into my shoulders.

"Thank you guys, come again."

"Be easy y'all," Jordan says, raising his arm and swaying it as he walks toward the door.

I look back one last time and wave goodbye to Pops and Ock with a fake smile, one which was mirrored back by both. Like looking at a still picture in a scrapbook, my memory of the bodega's off-blue tiled floor, rows of chips, candy, aisles of cans, and miscellaneous stuff that we never ventured toward contrasted what I was looking at now. It's all so unfamiliar as to what I remembered as a kid, everything is so small, but everything is in its place. Everything is where it's supposed to be ... yet, at the same time, it's all so different. I turn around and let the door close itself behind me as that last look around imprints itself in my head, slowly replacing the old still picture memory.

Jordan and I walk out and start heading toward the park.

"Damn this shit takes me back." He sniffs the sandwiches through the bag. "Man, das some good shit."

"Don't sniff our sandwiches like that."

"Nah," he continues to sniff them, "you was the one dat wanted our shit to touch."

"Yeah," I say, "I'm regretting that now."

"Y'know…"

I look at him and shake my head. This is exactly what we used to do in the old days after school at the bodega. A trip down memory lane greets us, only—like the bodega—things aren't like they used to be. The lane in front of us is filled with newspapers, wet and soaked into the pavement of the sidewalk by a suspicious puddle. The nuts and leaves from above had fallen to earth to meet their demise within the Timbs's dominion, as Jordan puts it. A wild, ongoing game of Jenga with garbage bags riddled portions of the sidewalk. Memory itself is a filter of perspective. Was it always like this? Or maybe I'm just looking at it differently now. That's why I hate coming back.

"…And she got a fat ass too, no funny shit."

"Hmm."

"Yo, you listening?"

"Huh?"

"Bruh."

"Nah yeah, you got a girl now?" I ask.

"Well, she ain't *my* girl," Jordan steps back, "cuz she ain't really all dat smart."

"Right."

A BUTTER ROLL · 51

A crossing of two blocks, juxtaposed the ones we had walked. They were clean and garbage-less. Walking through, Jordan points out the new businesses, the new buildings, and the new people moving in. He lamented the closing of the Jamaican spot around the corner with the "*fuego* jerk chicken and dumplings." He had even volunteered to work there for free if they'd just stay in business. Obviously, that didn't work. A bit down the block, we see a newly established café on the opposite side from the park. The café banner atop the storefront says *Café Moderno*.

"Maaann, if gentrification had a signature architecture, it would be this." Jordan points at the black borders of a mostly glass front.

The store is definitely out of character for the neighborhood. The sunlight pierces fiercely into the inside, showcasing the small hexagonal white floor tiles placed interchanged with black ones. There's a marble counter and behind that what seems to be a grill. The prices were laid out in a hanging, dark maho—

"*Six dollars* for a bacon egg and cheese? They be odeeinn' with the prices, bro." Jordan points to the item below beverages. "Bro. Coffee. Two beans and a half."

"What used to be here before this?" I ask.

"This used to be a—uh—"

"Hmm?" I look at Jordan, swaying my hand in front of his face, signaling him to continue.

"I'on even remember anymore," he shakes his head and walks into the park, "not dat it matters now anyways."

I follow along after him, crossing the street and stepping over garbage and a bunch of purple accented fliers on the floor. We sit at the empty bench, the café directly behind us separated only by the high black fence and the street. This is where Jordan and I would sit and talk shit for hours. It was a good spot overlooking the entirety of the park. A summer day like this would usually have the park full of kids playing. Back then, it was filled with a bunch of young'uns playing and hooping, and moms gossiping and talking shit. But it's all empty now. The park now consisted of broken swings, oxidized iron pipes of the jungle gym, and the locked little building that provided bathrooms for all those who would use it. The greenery had overgrown past its boundaries, and you could still see the leaves of last autumn mixed with the overgrowth of spring still stuck to the cracking, lumped pavement. I think back to my memories here after school. Was it always like this? I guess it kinda always was, to be honest, but just not to this extent—just not this desolate … and especially not on such a nice summer day.

Tightly clutching the same purple accented white flier in his hand, a lone, motionless, homeless man sleeps two benches away from us … or is dead? A rat and a squirrel chase each other under the man's bench, slap boxing ongoing, to then hide behind the foliage. Candles stacked like troops litter the basketball court—a tribute to the senseless violence of those too ignorant within their circumstance, and those too unlucky to face said ignorance.

"It's been a good minute since you've been back." Jordan sits back on the bench and fondles his bag. "You see how different it is, bro?"

"Yeah." I put my hand in the bag and pass Jordan his sandwich. "Here."

"Summer day and no one's out." He swigs his Arizona.

"Kids have phones nowadays." I take out my sandwich and place the bag between us. "It's kinda early, too."

"You right." Jordan unwraps half the sandwich and bites into it ferociously, moaning and nodding his head as he chews. He breathes in deeply, holds it, and then breathes out. He looks to his left, stops moaning, and stares into the distance. His gaze fixes on a white woman with long, flowing, blonde hair, wearing a white, flowy runners suit. He follows her down the block as she runs down the street farther into where we came from. The wind, brushing along the garbage and leaves, follows in her steps just as closely as his gaze, leaving behind a cleaner street behind her. Looking down, he smiles, chuckles, then bites his sandwich.

"What?" I ask. It's probably something dirty. It always is.

"Fuck this sandwich good bro." He ignores me, and continues to bite into his sandwich as I unwrap my butter roll. He crushes the tinfoil paper into a ball and throws it into the black plastic bag, grabbing the rest of the sandwich with his bare hands. He pauses for a moment, then savors his last bite and breathes out.

...

"I guess das how things are now around here," he says.

"What?"

"You see the candles at the court?" He ignores me again.

"Yeah." I bite into the butter roll and with a mouthful, I continue, "What was it this time."

"Hmm," Jordan sits forward, elbows on knees stuffing his face, "some dumb shit."

"That's why we need to get this education," I continue.

"You say dat like our education makes us any better." Jordan sits back from his elbows on knees position and drinks his Arizona. "Our education don't make us any better, it just makes us aware, and das even worse."

"How?" I bite my butter roll again, eating half of it, leaving the other half untouched as I drink out my Arizona.

"Yeah, think about it, you see the environment we were raised in. You see the candles at the court, you see how the cops do us dirty 'round here, you see how everythin' 'round here risin'—rent, property taxes," he flails his arms toward the bodega's direction, "look at Ock, bro … at the … at the … b'dega, dude can't even make his rent unless he make a Pringles can like two beans. On one hand, we bein' pushed out, on another, we either die or stay down. An education don't give you the opportunity to fix it, just to leave it."

"So, let's leave it." I swig my Arizona and sit back on the bench.

"But this is home," he huffs out, and breathes in deeply and out again, "this is where we grew up at."

"*We're* home." I slap his chest with the back of my left hand and bring it back to my chest. "Us. You and Me."

"Dat's funny," he shakes his head and huffs his nose again, "nigga, you barely here to be sayin' dat corny shit."

"I know I haven't been here in a minute," I breathe out, "but you and your dad, I love y'all."

"Weird way of showin' it," he says.

He huffs his nose little by little until his smile comes out through a chuckle. He looks at me, shaking his head at my display of affection. He opens the Sour Power straws, bites one, and chews it down. He offers me some, which I refuse, as he continues to look forward to the street past the park. Suddenly turning his head to me, he is struck with wild realization.

"A—yoooo, dat sounded a lil sus bro," he chuckles, licking his lip and pouting pensively. "They always said dat Ivy,

A BUTTER ROLL · 55

higher education will make you think outside the box. Now I know what box they referrin' to."

"Wow."

"I knew going to Columbia was gon' make you batt, battymon," he laughs.

"Haven't you heard?" I joke around, "Homophobia is gay."

Jordan scrunches his face in confusion, stretching the corners of his mouth as he brings up another Sour Power straw to his face and bites it, keeping the same face of bizarre confusion throughout.

I explain, "Think about it. You conflate any sort of love between brethren as sexual. You look at two dudes and you automatically think they gay, maybe you're projecting yourself onto the world."

"Nah," he shakes his head, now looking down to the ground.

"Plus, why you in two grown men's business?" I flail my arms in question. "Sounds kinda gay to me."

"Nah bro, you prolly eat franks now too."

"Franks?"

"Hotdogs," he shoots back, looking at me again. "Damn nigga, you ain't got internet?"

"I know what franks are." I smile at the absurdity of our conversation. "Eating hotdogs is gay now? We can't enjoy shit, huh."

"Shit been gay. Out here gobblin' glizzies."

We laugh in unison as he playfully pushes me. It was always like this. As kids we'd sit here and at the very end of it all, no matter what it was, it would just be jokes. Didn't matter how raw the problems were or how serious or how heated our conversations ever got … it would all end with jokes. Of course, now we're adults, and no amount of joking can remedy our adult problems. I guess he's right in that matter—being aware makes it worse, but wouldn't you rather know either way?

A still silence casts over the park, the birds' chirps drowning inaudibly in the background.

...

"How's daddy?" I break the silence. Jordan's father wasn't my biological father, but he'd raise me as one. He was a terrible cook, but he at least gave us something with actual nutrition after going to the store after school.

"He's...," Jordan pauses, his smile turning ambiguously serious or nonchalant, "man ... he's ... alright. Y'know how it is."

...

"He asks about you from time to time," Jordan continues.

"Yeah," I say with guilt. I hold the butter roll in my hand. I hadn't visited in a while, nor did I call or text or—as he'd often describe—send a pigeon.

...

"They got this new building they constructin' right up front." Jordan licks his lips, sharply breathing out air into an ambiguously veiled smile. "Shit bothers him in the morning. Shit bothers me too."

...

"Nevermind."

"I mean we here right now. Maybe I can come see him for a bit."

Jordan looks at me sideways and shakes his head. "He—he at work."

"Yeah ... you're right. Man—"

"But nah," Jordan says as he pulls out his phone, "it's twelve past eleven, we should start heading out."

"Yeah." I look down at my watch and gulp down the remainder of my Arizona. We stand up and walk outside of the park to the trashcan in front of the entrance. Jordan downs three straws in his mouth, throwing the wrapper and both of our Arizona bottles into the bag all together. He tosses it into the garbage. I look down at my half-eaten butter roll and chuck it in as well and signal to the train station.

"You ain't finish your butter roll?" he asks while chewing.

"Nah, it tastes different."

CHAPTER 4

THE NEW YORKERS

ALEX
[Manhattan Bound M Train Platform]
[Queens]
[11:12 a.m.]

The black borders contrast off-white tiles, enclosing the purple-accented white advertisement. In it was a picture of a woman with kids huddled into a hug, smiling. The words above her read:

"*As per established NYC rent control guidelines, it is against the law for landlords to randomly increase your rent. If your landlord is randomly increasing your rent, please notify the NYC tenant hotline: 1-800-555-RENT*

Tenants have rights. We stand with you.

Sponsored by the NYC Department Against Homelessness"

"Ma'—am ... lem—me get a ... *doler*"—cough—cough—"excuse me, please."

The homeless man leans on the downwardly slanted and segmented seating area. Slouched against the beam, his legs hang macabre-like, as if he'd been hit by a car, contorted and bent in different ways. The train stations in Queens had been like this for a year now. All throughout—

"Excuse me."

—Queens the rate of homeless—

"Can I get a *doler*?"

"I only have card," I lie promptly with a gentle smile. "Sorry."

"Issokay," the homeless man says, "thank you for not ignorin' me."

Damn … I really ain't shit if I don't give this old man a dollar. I swing my backpack to the front and pretend to fondle it. Man … I ain't shit. I already knew where my cash was, but I had to make it seem like I miraculously found something in it to give to him. I act pensive, looking up at the ceiling and around as I feel for absolutely nothing in particular in my bag. I take out four dollars and hand it to him.

"Thank you."

I smile at the man and walk farther down into the platform. The rumble of the train emanates from deep within the tunnel before the two front lights show themselves from the tunnel's horizon with a red sign above it. A slight wind brews as it approaches; a slight wind that turns into a gust of hot wind as it passes, swaying my hair slightly. NYC summer days are hell. The days aren't ever really—

Da kunk-kunk da kunk—kunk da kunk—kunk skreeeeeeeeeee Phsssh

—hot. They're just so humid … always messing up my hair.

The screeches of the train resonate around the station as it slows and gradually comes to a complete stop. The automatic doors open abruptly, releasing an air-conditioned breeze that battles the summer musk of the station. Before entering the train, I peep the half-full, half-empty car split in the middle, juxtaposing the rest of the packed cars. Lemme guess, a homeless person in the corner smelling like ass? Should I take my chances with the stank of whatever is in there or with directly smelling armpits in a crowded car? Hmmm. Sigh, I'll take my chances.

Four people leave the train as eleven more enter it. I enter it on the side most full and see that my prediction is laying on the corner of the opposite side of the car. The air feels stale but doesn't smell as bad as I thought it would. A small tinge of sweat, ass, and destitution couples the cool air of the car, but hey … at least it ain't hot. Liquid pools at the bottom of the homeless person's seat, and like a lake with multiple streams, the pool had flowed to all corners of the car. The farthest stream stops right before the pole that separates the very middle of the car. As the inconspicuous "liquid" teeters ever so slightly past it, people move further and further away, of course, blatantly disgusted by the liquid. They encroach closer and closer toward themselves on the far extremity of the train, huddling into a concentrated ball.

The speaker system blasts:

"This is a Manhattan Bound M Local Train."
"The next stop is Forty-Sixth Street."
"Stand clear of the closing doors please."
Ding dong
The doors begin to close, but pivot and open again.
…
Ding dong
The door closes.

The still silence of the train dissipates to a rambunctious popping and grinding as it begins to move. As it speeds, the sound melts into white noise coupled with sporadic *kunks*, a New Yorker's lullaby. It wouldn't be strange to find someone in a late afternoon swaying at its cadence's behest, deep in a trance induced sleep. Of course, you'd be a wallet and bag short if you actually fell asleep, but there's something therapeutic about riding the train after a long day at work. Definitely not in the morning though or midday … and certainly not in this one.

Upon movement, the liquid from the far side of the train shifts and displaces itself farther, adding to the volume of the incoming stream past the pole. More and more people shift over, a variety of scents and musks muddled together in the confined space of half the car. The cool air alleviates the symptoms of the stank but as nauseating as it is, I huff my nose and turn my face to avert it from the now-near armpits.

Outside the train the beam of lights within the tunnels zooms past my eyes, illuminating old graffiti tags. It wouldn't surprise me if some hipster company repurposed the inside of the tunnels and sprayed them with art, hiding away some of the history of it. It sounds like something they'd do.

There was never a bleak moment while riding the train during the summer. It is always so wild and so strange that you might even think it's all curated, a deliberate façade. I once saw a squirrel and a rat fight over a half-eaten pizza slice. Like … how wildly random is that?

It's hard to think that there isn't someone orchestrating all of the madness that happens underground as some sort of social experiment. Maybe there are CIA agents in the control rooms of the MTA monitoring how we'd react to the absurdities they manufacture. Regardless of it all, it almost seems unreal the things and characters you see on the train. Riding the train, in a twisted way, is a way to market yourself. You act accordingly. You show what you want to show. It's where we put our most curated public self into effect. Of course, even the advertisements were curated too ... there was *nothing* more curated than the advertisements in trains.

I look up at the overhead advertisements running throughout the entire length of the train. There's a bright orange banner displaying a long-bearded goat in yoga pants. "Goat-tea & Yoga."—a small company created by the uber hipsters that now inhabit Astoria, but was later bought out, like everything, by the conglomerate monopoly titan, *Amagone*. Now it's a subsidiary consisting of the weirdest and most expanding of goat services. They used to offer goat tea, but now it's other goat products. My NYU friends really like their goat yogurt. It's made with raw goat's milk, which *was* originally prohibited in the NYC markets due to ... very *obvious* health concerns. To make it even worse, they process it in a cramped warehouse right here in the city. Of course, now it's legal. With the corporate bribes and the ever-growing market, the city saw that they could make more money than harm by taxing it instead of prohibiting it. There was a chain of scandals surrounding these corporate bribes to city council to allow less restrictive distributions and hide animal cruelty reports, amongst other things, but nothing happened. I mean ... who actually cares, really?

Now, they drone goats in cages to your "urban" rooftop yoga session, where at the end, there's an instructor that can help you milk your own goat for you to make ice cream. I still can't believe they're allowed to sell that diarrhea inducing yogurt ... all with a goat's face on it. And they're making a killing, the advertisement itself being a testament to the new overspending, avocado-toast-eating demographic of Queens.

"*Ahhhheeeee.*"

Ah shit. The stream passes the pole and touches a man's foot as he shrieks in excruciating agony. Oh the horror of your sneakers touching a bit of piss, as if any other public surface in this city is any cleaner. His actions cause a reaction that causes another reaction that causes another reaction that ... well ... leads to a pregnant lady being elbowed. The pregnant lady talks shit under her breath as she holds on to the pole with six other people. Her eyes fix on everyone sitting down. They find refuge from her gaze on their phones, avoiding eye contact. She looks around, her gaze, and everyone else's gaze, oscillating with the lack of each other's presence. I guess degeneracy is truly the way to go.

 She rubs her stomach, pretending to do so nonchalantly ... like c'mon, you know they see it. No one budges. No one cares. I look through the window toward the next car to see if any space is available and find that it is all crowded. It was morning rush hour on a summer day and the unemployed have brunches to attend. Not many people get on a train in Queens to hop off ... in Queens ... well not this part of Queens at least. Amagone had opened its massive new headquarters encompassing entire quadrants, and I mean, *entire* quadrants. It vastly changed the layout of how the city and the people moved. Before its unholy presence, the main traffic for workers was from Queens to Manhattan. That being said, most folks still work in Manhattan, or "the city." Always hated that: "the city." *We live in the city* ... maybe it's not the quirky "I'm a New Yorker now" aesthetic influencer New York, but it's the city nonetheless. The huge headquarters now presented a shift with a large concentration of jobs in the area leading more people from Manhattan into Queens, which means I get to see more influencer-wannabe hoes living off of daddy's paycheck and lifestyle Youtubers redefining what "the city" is. I'm tired of hearing "O—M—G I just discovered this hidden gem in NYC! It used to be kinda sus, but now it's super cool." They got the street art, the graffiti, and Amagone and—

The train starts to slow down as it comes into the station.

Skreeeeeeeeeee

My entire body shuffles to the right. I pivot my feet and dig my shoes into the ground supporting my body against the door, and the overhead pole ... thingy ... whatever those are called. An armpit softly grazes the back of my head, caressing it lovingly. Aww ... how affectionate.

Da kunk-kunk da kunk—kunk da kunk—kunk skreeeeeeeeeee Phsssh

The speaker system blasts:

"This is Forty-Sixth Street."

"Transfer is available to the R Train."

The train makes a complete stop. The doors open as people stare at the inside of the car, some catch on and walk to another car, or enter through the full side. Three people enter through the middle, stepping over the liquid, and sit down. They immediately realize the reason for a half empty car as they quickly cover their noses. They stand up and walk toward the cluttered side of the cart, their very presence wafting the stink brought about by their very being. They had broken an unspoken rule, right up there with ignoring the Jesus freaks and the homeless beggars: never come through the empty side of a car in a full train. It's obvious that there's a reason for it, yet they did it anyway. Probably new to the neighborhood.

Amagone is a job hotspot for new graduates, meaning the area is also seeing a lot of new residents. Amagone uses local and city subsidies fueled by native taxpayer dollars to create jobs within their campus. Those jobs mostly end up going to privileged, once suburban–now "urban" ... transplants, they call them. I like to call them what they truly are: gentrifiers. They often come with an idealized version of living "in the city."

Savory is a lot of their disappointment when they find that "the city" was not like any of the trash sit-coms they watched as kids. You can't live in a huge apartment with a cook's salary. You can't habitually party every Friday night and go out for brunch the next morning. The streets aren't clean and the city isn't this vast playground of lights and watered down culture; its very existence is simply a way to entertain and feed them. In fact—for them, honestly—"the city" turned out to be rather small, ranging from midtown to downtown, perhaps Williamsburg, Bushwick, Long Island City ... or Coney Island if they're feeling adventurous. Their worldview of the boroughs is only as wide as their aesthetics are concerned. If it isn't "cool" or "trendy" or "up and coming" ... they aren't there. I know this firsthand from my NYU friends who stupidly believed their lives would be reminiscent of that.

"This is a Manhattan Bound M Local Train."

"The next stop is Steinway Street."

"Stand clear of the closing doors please."

Ding dong.

The doors begin to close, but pivot and open again.

...

Ding dong

The doors resist closing.

...

Ding dong

The doors fail to close again. Who's holding the doors?

The train conductor's buzzy intercom blasts: "*Stzozp hzoldzinzg tzhez dzoorz. Thze kzidzs inz thze bazzck stzop pzlayzing wzithz thzem dzoors.*"

Ding dong

The doors close and the train begins to slowly pick up speed. Behind a very tainted and scratched window, the last thing I see before being consumed in the pale white lights of the train in the tunnel is an advertisement for the newest season of a trash sitcom ... you could tell.

The poster advertisement featured an expensive Brooklyn brownstone with two white women centered in the middle, sitting on the stoops looking nonchalantly at either side, smiling, probably daydreaming. There were three sprinkles of diversity on there—what I will assume is a *very* light-skinned Indian lady, maybe Latina, and the most racially ambiguous brown-paper-bag Black woman they could find. The last sprinkle was a dark-skin Black man, who—although being several shades darker—is the brother of the Black woman on the show and plays the love interest for both white women. What a tragedy. I think I've heard about this show. I just didn't see the name of it well, nor can I remember the name of it.

Girls who move into the city and have a bunch of sex while they live in expensive apartments financed by influencer life and daddy's money. That's basically the show. Or is that another show? What does it matter? It's the same archetype. Gentrification is continuously getting a show made about your city, and it's never about you. It's always about someone else trying to find themselves, while the rest of us become lost in their attempt. We become nothing more—

"This is Steinway Street."

"Transfer is available to the R Train."

—than fuel for their needs of adventure and to become "cultured," as if we're nothing more than the bacteria they use to make those fucking goat yogurts.

The liquid had shifted more and more into the crowded portion of the train, leading to people pushing farther away from the liquid as possible. Shouting ensues as people shove and violate each other's personal space. At that same moment, the homeless man at the opposite corner of the train explodes with anger, "*Shut up. Shut up. I'm tryna sleep.*"

The speaker system blasts:

"This is a Manhattan Bound Local Train."

"The next stop is Thirty-Sixth Street—Amagone East."

"Stand clear of the closing doors please."

Ding dong

The car doors close, and everyone falls silent. The vanguard of the crowded group wince as their white, low-top shoes make mild contact with the streams. They huddle together to discuss.

"Should we call the conductor or the platform police?" one of them says.

"No. After all that's happened this summer? I'm trying to keep my job, man."

"Well … it isn't for *no* reason."

"We won't have to," the ponytail, Bob Marley shirt wearing guy says with confidence. "Next stop is Thirty-Sixth Street."

The train sways rapidly in the tunnel till the light dissipates the darkness as we enter the station. Figures dressed in blue blur past my eyes as the train begins to slow down. The train slows—

Da kunk-kunk da kunk—kunk da kunk—kunk skreeeeeeeeeee Phsssh

"This is Thirty-Sixth Street—Amagone East."

—steadily until coming to a complete stop. The humming resonating through the entirety of the train pauses as it powers down and becomes stagnant.

The speaker system blasts:

"This is a message from the New York City Police Department: All suspicious persons and packages can and will be subject to random search by the police. Thank you and have a great day."

What a beautifully timed reminder. The train doors open as I move to the side. People make their way out of the car and onto the platform, swerving out of the approaching officers' way. They enter through the middle door and nonchalantly stand on top of the stream of liquid on the floor. They look around, their nostrils flaring from the swamp ass smell emanating from the side of the car. Clearly understanding the situation, they put on gloves and masks, signaling the remaining officer on the platform who then, with a gesture, signals the conductor to stay put.

"Finally, they'll take this guy out of here," one gentrifier says, tiptoeing over the streams of liquid.

Both officers walk over and loom above the homeless man, stepping directly over the large lake of liquid. One of the officers taps the man on the shoulder. No reaction. The officers repeatedly tap him on his shoulder yielding no reaction as the homeless man lays restless.

"C'mon. I know you're awake. You can't be here," one of the officers says. "Get up."

The homeless man lies there as we watch, hoping the officers will just leave him alone. They won't. The officers impatiently tap the homeless man, waiting a moment to then tap him again. The homeless man opens his eyes, defeated, and sits up on the chair. Instinctively, everyone takes their cameras out to record the interaction. The beginning of the summer was filled with police brutality, a lengthy investigation into NYPD arrest quotas, corruption, and a whole bunch of other pre-existent, obvious shit people were blind to. It was even more prevalent around Brooklyn, but all around it has been a very eventful summer for the city. There was a citywide protest and calls for the disbandment of the Amagone police. That lasted about two weeks, and then ... nothing. No legislation. Nothing changed. Of course, nothing changed. Everything went back to "normal." Except now we have protest veterans cashing in their protest cards at any sign of consequence or criticism.

I swing my backpack in front of me and reach for my camera to start taking pictures of the interaction. One of the officers looks toward the crowded side and sees the barrage of lenses pointed toward him and his partner and turns his back to the camera. Probably trying to hide the interactions—fucking pig.

"You can't be here," the other officer repeats, "you have to get up."

"I'm tryin' to sleep," the homeless man defends. "I'm just tryin' to—"

The policeman that turned his back to the cameras grabs the shoulder of the homeless man, prompting the homeless man to scoff him off. Taking offense, the officer places his hand forcefully back on the homeless man's shoulder who begins pleading, "*No, don't touch me. Don't Touch me. Please!*"

Both officers grab the homeless man by his arms and ragged backpack, shuffling their weight around to get him out the seat. They stretch his clothing in the process, while one officer changes his grip to behind the homeless man's neck, squeezing it tight to get a better hold. He lets out a scream, "No, please. I just want to sleep!"

They haul the man out of the seat, thrashing him on the pole of the far side of the car and placing him against the outside of the train window. Struggling to get on his dragging feet, the man begins to cry as they push their bodies against his and throw him onto the ground of the platform. He thrashes about, now sobbing, "I just want to sleep!"

The ponytail gentrifier with his phone out filming says, "Oh my god, look what they're doing to that poor guy."

You—what did you expect? You thought the NYPD was just going to be nice to a homeless man within campus grounds? That they were just going to be nice to him? *This is Thirty-Sixth Street, the beginning of the Amagone campus.* The area from this point until the East River—including train stations—is Amagone property, and based off a deal done with the city mayor and the city council, it is to be continuously guarded by NYPD officers to ensure "safety." Really, the word "safety" is just coded language to get rid of undesirables. At the end of the day, the deal was nothing more than just some bullshit made to protect the aesthetic and common interest of the businesses in the area. After the housing crisis two years ago left thousands of families homeless or near-homeless in the city, there was a rise in robberies, violence, and the creation of "bumsvilles" in local parks—but the city couldn't have that. God forbid they ever listen to experts and do the right thing.

More officers from other train cars come running to help the officers on top of the homeless man. One officer, a purple and white band on his left arm, instructs the others to prop the man up on his feet and take him outside the platform. They readily manhandle him and drag him up the stairs of the station as the station platform clears itself. The same officer faces the crowded side of the car and says, "Sorry guys please go about your day, we will take care of the situation and ensure the safety of the man apprehended."

Apprehended? Apprehended for what? What law did he break?

He smiles blankly and raises his hand up, signaling the conductor. The doors shut immediately and everyone in their silence continues on their phone, uploading the video to social media. The strange clattering of thumbs and keyboard noises drowns the clanking sounds of the train and the machine's hum, all encompassed in this awkward, ambivalent, live silence. Ponytail breaks the silence: "That was horrible."

Wow. Just a few seconds ago you were—

He continues, "What should I say in this post?"

Wow. It's like that? You want the man to be removed, but you don't like how he was removed? No. That's not it. You don't care. You just care that you look like you care. No one really does—not even the Department Against Homelessness cares for the homeless, or about people losing their homes, or about people in general. It's just a farce. For them, advocating for the pain of others is just a way for social capital, to look cool, to virtue signal, to seem as if they're making a difference in society.

The speaker system blasts:

"This is a Manhattan Bound M local train."

"The next stop is Amagone Central."

Half of the car leaves, leaving more space for us remaining there. Ponytail guy gets off with his entourage, still thinking what to say. That's how it is though. The less fortunate are just an aesthetic to be used and consumed, to bolster another's image. They march one day, then go to lunch, dinner, whatever, and then back home. The next day is just another day. They only care as much as their aesthetic is concerned. It's all a show. Especially when they even benefit from your misfortunes, then they feel more obligated to come out and support. It's like how rich people send their kids to Africa on mission trips. Their kids get their hair braided, they feed starving children, take a bunch of pictures to show to their friends and family members. They get to mention it to their friends and their kids get to use it as a way to beef up their resume for college. That's ponytail man and his ilk. It's all hopeless, especially when things are really hard around the city.

In the past two years, after Amagone solidified its grasp on Queens—and the entire city really—everything has been slipping. Barely any entry-level jobs for the community, everything's expensive, everything's corporatized, homelessness everywhere, rent rising, and people that only care for it all as far as their aesthetic is concerned. The city is getting harder to live in. That's why I started a project coalition connecting the city to people, so we can converse and share how things are going in the NYC community: how things are changing, how things affect us, and how they're thriving through it all. Abel thinks it's stupid, but then again, Abel thinks everything is stupid. He always says "a hashtag only makes a revolution obsolete" and that "people are unwilling to do the ugly actions that'd lead to change." But I think that it's a really beautiful thing to get people together to solve a common issue. Plus, it's become a beacon of support for people in the city at large.

Now that I think about it. I need to take more pictures for the Instagram page.

"This is Forty-Seventh to Fiftieth Street—Rockefeller Center."

"Transfer is available to the B, D, and F train."

I snap out of it as the system calls the station, and quickly jump off the train and onto the platform, following the outward rush of people moving in and out of the train car, onto the platform and up the stairs.

"This is a downtown M local train."

"The next stop is Forty-Second Street—Bryant Park."

"Stand Clear of the Closing Doors Please."

Alright. Now I just need to go uptown toward the park. I walk up to the upper level and see the multitude of people zipping past one another, their minds only occupied with their destination.

I take out my phone and message Abel: "I'mma be there in 15-20. Just wait in front of the Theater."

I weave past the multitude of people, up the stairs and onto the vast floor on the upper level to transfer to the B train. On top of the platform, amidst the rushing of people, my eyes catch something. I take out my camera and snap a photo.

A homeless woman sits underneath the same advertisement I'd seen earlier featuring the expensive Brooklyn brownstones. Reading the title, it hits me. Above the homeless woman's head, in bold yellow script, the title of the show displays itself proudly: "The New Yorkers."

CHAPTER 5

A SUS REUNION

ABEL
[Near the Great Lawn, Central Park]
[Manhattan]
[11:56 a.m.]

"Yeerrrr," my scream penetrates the lawn's atmosphere, turnin' heads, but reaching only the ears of those culturally competent enough to decipher it as a greeting as opposed to, what it would sound like to the untrained ear, an incoherent cry. A dog, recognizin' his own kind, barks at me as I pass by 'im. He sniffs my feet as his owner takes 'im away walkin'. It's an extremely hot day today, which means I'll have to graze shoulders with far too many people for my likin', but don't worry reader, there's no Rona in this timeline. As such, the park is packed with people basking and soaking up the sun to get tanner, an aesthetic now more popularized by the big booty melanin shorties in the video and the general idea dat "maybe if I tan enough, push my overlined lips forward, and put these hoop earrings on, I'll be a nigga too." If the park were a grill grate, they'd be the Perdue chicken trynna hide their pale skin, forever ungrateful for and ignorant of the fruits of its existence. Damn I'm good at narration. Lemme write dat down.

I swing my backpack open, take out my journal, and write down the truth dat I hope offends many:

"Blanquitos trynna be negritos."

"Yerrrrrrr," a troglodyte lookin' muh'fucka shouts back.

I thank god everyday it's not a matin' call. Jordan extends his hands above his head, standin' shoulder width apart. Next to 'im is Marcus already shakin' his head and smirking, a gesture dat forever exemplifies his overall attitude and rejection of our shenanigans. Even before getting into Columbia, he had always worn his dumb disappointed smile. I hate it ... he thinks he's better than us all, and now dat he's all Ivy League now, he prolly is. Once they take dat first step on the upwards mobility ladder, they start to move different. Like my father, Marcus never visits, rarely calls or respond to texts ... He just stays up there in his ivory tower, workin' toward makin' the steps to gain a wider view, not realizin' dat it looks as shitty up there as it does down here, but oh man are the couches up there comf'table.

"What's goodie, gang." I extend my hand out to dap Jordan, firmly claspin' his first date sweaty palms and bringin' 'im in for a brotherly, no homo, no incest, embrace. It's been a minute, not gon' lie, kinda 'bout to tear up. I hold 'im at arm's length shakin' 'im, fake wipin' the tears off my eyes as I contort the face of dat of a lost child now happily rejoined with his mother. But unlike a mother, I actually could care less to see Jordan. I see 'im all the time. I dare his ugly ass to hit me wit some dumb shit like: oh you never come visit bro and I'm always here in el Bronx. Like, man shut yo bitch ass up. Actin' like dat shit wasn't just a courtesy visit from the weak ass dicklivery service he runs. Dat being said, though I've seen 'im time and time again, it's quite different to see these two faces together ... I missed my brothers, man. They a lil uglier than I remember tho. I face Marcus's quadratic slope of a hairline and extend my hand. "Damn bro, you straight outta Rikers or sum? You look dusty, chopped."

"I got a cut like three weeks ago." Marcus, clearly out of practice, gives me one of those soft half daps, half handshakes. I look at 'im strangely and pick up my hand to try again, which is met with a mediocre, yet acceptable dap. Prolly shakin' hands now instead of dappin' it up. Like damn, give me a real dap. Fuck dat bum ass handshake, we not capitalists yet, we gotta fuck up a single mom's day first.

"Well, fire 'im nigga cuz you look homeless," I look closely at his lineup and then at his face, and, like Maury, decide dat it is *not* the source of his chopp'dness, "but damn bro, even wit the cut, you'd still be a lil ugly either way."

"Wow." Marcus smirks and shakes his head again.

His smirk slightly turned into a small chuckle which sat uncomfortably on his face, almost like it wasn't even supposed to be there or as if it hadn't been there in a while. Well, damn. Dat's new. He never chuckles. He was a master at dat. Ever since high school, amidst all our bullshit, all our fuck ups, and all the dumb shit we ever did ... All this man could ever muster was a smirk and a disappointed look. He was like the father I never had. But deadass, he never chuckles. Aww ... he missed me. Pause. Or maybe, he's been up there for too long. Up there with those dumb fuck "intellectuals" dat can't tell a joke in fear of losing their air of "wokeness." Can't even say the word "bitch" near 'em. I can already hear 'em say: "Oh how dare you sir, why sir don't you know dat's misogynistic?" I've courted many women and not once, in the midst of my strokes and me talkin 'bout beatin' the pussy, has she ever stopped me to analyze the implications of the usage of the word. So is it really dat important? Or maybe I gotta start datin' these academia women. I heard the pussy has the proper knowledge to set a brother free ... sum called the savior complex. Either way, it's some scholarly pussy.

"We been here for a bit; Alex not here yet tho." Jordan looks toward the west side of the Great Lawn. Wow he can use his brain now. I mean, he used a semicolon correctly. Alex prolly taking the M train to get here, droppin' 'er off on the west side of the lawn. I'm surprised Jordan's brain can even compute dat. I've never known Jordan to be able to use his head for anything other than fuckin'. Reader, there's a pun there.

"College clearly made you smarter, huh." I look around fake confused, lookin' for a sign of a yet-to-appear Alex. Oh where might she be?

"Eat a Frank." Jordan, ironically, sucks his teeth and makes a face like he just smelled his breath on his upper lip. He looks at his phone and then up.

"I'on eat pork cuz y'know." I put my fist up in brethren solidarity which was met with suckin' teeths. I signal toward the westbound path outside of the lawn. "Trains comin' from Uptown and Queens are delayed today. She messaged me she'd be here in fifteen."

"Today?" Jordan shakes his head. "Trains be delayed every day. I be trynna drop dick—"

Ewww. Reader, I'm so sorry this bum is sayin' things like this and you have to read it. I try to keep my perspective PG for you. I'm sorry. Very ghetto.

"—shorty be wearin' red all sometimes, y'feel me—"

Oh he's not done yet. *Lalalalalalala.*

"—but I hate havin' to go to the Bronx *from* Brooklyn and then havin' to get. Nah."

"You didn't have to say any of that," Marcus says, lookin' at his watch with a concerned face.

"First off, I ain't hear nun of dat, but if you fuckin' with Bronx females, *they* fucked *you*, not the other way around." I stop 'im in his tracks, pointin' two fingers, fingertips knuckle's width apart, at his chest. Fuck outta here. I'on really fuck with nun of 'em dummy hoes up in the Bronx, but ain't no one gon' say the Bronx gets fucked. "Them Bronx girls will fuck you up, stop playin' with 'em. Fuck with some Brooklyn hoes, I hear they still fuck you with 'em bumass 2013 huaraches on instead of timbs."

Jordan sucks his teeth immaculately, proof of his frank eatin' habits, while agitatingly vibratin' his hands up and down, "Shut the fuck up, like damn…"

Jordan. Check. Smiling, I open my backpack and, like a titty, fondle around the contents and reach to the very bottom and pull out my leather-bound journal. With my clown brethrens, you never know when inspiration will hit you. I signal to the Delacorte Theater, startin' us off on our way over there. We walk with and past a multitude of people as we find a spot for us to sit at as we wait for Alex.

We sit at one end of a long bench in front of the Theater. Jordan, lettin' gravity do the work for 'im and droppin' 'imself onto the bench, creates a crazy vibration dat clearly bothers the old lady sittin' at the other end of the bench, but since we deadass look like the human portrayal of the worst synonym of "urban," she remains silent. I sit in between Jordan and Marcus, who had sat 'imself with all the delicate poise of a lady. We sat close enough to each other, but not enough where our manhood would be questioned. We spread our legs to catch the subtle warm breeze to cool our hot balls, like every man does, and should, reader.

It's been a minute since we all got together like this to chop it up and chill. We've all been "busy." Marcus never comes back "home" even tho he technically lives here. Technically, in the sense dat up there is a different world. He prolly be kicking it with them white suburban kids ... no wonder he's talkin' a lil weird. Jordan's in school. Should definitely ask 'im how it's going, but he clearly ain't takin' dat shit too seriously if he got time to go up to the Bronx to run his STD delivery service. Alex, on the other hand, is always going around the city with 'er NYU film friends tryin' to make lil movies and disrespectin' my homies in Congress who are tryin' to take they reproductive rights away. Our schedules never coincide, until today.

"Bro, tell me how Marcus's auntie was out here—"

"Rubbin' 'er son's head?" I finish Jordan's sentence. Aww, we so cute together, finishing each other's sentences and what not.

"You probably shouldn't go around mentioning that so loudly and publicly," Marcus comments defeatedly.

"How you know dat?" Jordan ignores 'im, askin' me how I could possibly know sum so blatantly obvious.

"I thought we all knew? This the new baby, right?" I chuckle. "Cuz she was preggy some time ago. Lil man should be 'bout a year now or sum."

"How you—wha—so no one said anything?" Jordan scrunches his face. "We just not supposed to talk about it."

"Stop." Marcus shakes his head.

"I mean we can't be talkin' 'bout dat out *here*," I say.

"Why?" Jordan asks.

"It's offensive," Marcus says.

"How?" Jordan asks.

He remains speechless as he waves his left hand and massages his brow.

"It's one of those things where you just know it's offensive," I joke, "but you can't really say why."

"I was the only one who ain't know this?"

"I mean, you was there when we talked about it dat last time," I say, "you even commented dat she looked fatter when you saw her walkin' to the bodega."

"So Abel, what have you been up to?" Marcus changes the subject.

"Straight chillin' bro, like … y'know how it is, me and [redacted] reppin', we mobbin' deep in the trenches." I jokingly smile, while Jordan chuckles a bit and Marcus shakes his head.

I would love to be the beauty dat is a walkin' stereotype. It would give me the ignorance needed to live a life without nuance. Dat's "gang" life for sure. Funny enough, some of the people I knew in gangs now, [redacted] or otherwise, were going to college, trade school, or buildin' businesses, rapping or some other shit. It's 2027, weed's legalized, crime is down, new encoded security and RFID chips makes scamming harder. They got robot dogs scannin' faces in the streets. In short, all this gangbangin' not paying any bills whatsoever. Shit's corny anyways.

I continue, "Nah I've just been chillin' for real. Took a lil break from school."

Marcus relaxes on his seat, looking up toward the top of the theatre building and squintin' his eyes at the sunlight. "You still doing comedy?"

"Comedy?" Jordan questions.

"Yeah, he's been doing it since high school." Marcus looks down at his watch and then looks at me.

"What? How have I not heard this?" Jordan asks as he points at my journal. "So what's dat?"

"Oh this?" I flaunt my journal, smiling and gesturing it in front of 'em nonchalantly. "This is my jokes journal."

"What?" Jordan asks.

"I do jokes in clubs now, so I gotta have a lil joke pad like all the greats," I say smugly thinkin' they'll be surprised, but no.

Marcus makes an undecipherable look of approval or indifference, while Jordan opens his eyes and makes about the same face. I sigh and continue, "What have you guys been up to?"

"I've been fucking bitches in the Bronx nigga, I just told you," Jordan says tiltin' his head up to the sun and closin' his eyes.

"School and work," Marcus says plainly.

"School and work." I choose to entertain Marcus. I might catch an ear infection or sum, if I hear Jordan any longer. "Word? Even choir boys get more action than you. Is dat all you did over the summer?"

"Yeah, I was working for this startup earlier in the summer and I was also taking a class or two."

"What you do there in them startups?" Jordan asks while rubbin' his eyes shut.

"Anything and everything they tell me to do," Marcus sighs, lookin' down at his watch and back up, "but mostly just business analytics, kinda like consulting."

"Oh so you the big steppa now huh. So dat's why you never holla at ya boys no more?" I pat my chest and Jordan's, startlin' 'im to reopen his closed eyes bewildered, look at me, then closin' 'em again. I continue, "You out there putting in work without relaxin'?"

"Workin' 'em cheeks off," Jordan adds.

"Yeah, I'm just…" Marcus pauses as he joins me and turns, face deadpan, to look at Jordan for a second. He continues, "…tired."

"Of course you tired," Jordan opens his eyes, blinkin' rapidly, "cuz you ain't comin' round and chillin' and shit, you always at work or up there grindin'."

"Yeah dat's why you out here talkin' type weird," I poke. I have to poke. Dat shit's been botherin' me this whole time now. Y'on gotta code switch wit us bro. Just be yourself. Speak "normally."

"Like what?" Marcus shoots back quickly.

"With an accent," Jordan chimes in witout hesitation. So I'm not trippin', I'm not the only one dat noticed it. "I noticed it at the park earlier near ya crib, but I ain't say anythin'."

"It's more like witout an accent than wit one," I further explain, "you can't call flavorless a flavor."

"I mean…" Marcus starts, now self-conscious of his voice, "I think I speak normal."

"You are talking in full like this," Jordan jokes, "you saying every word and syllable clear as fuck."

"Nah bro. A lil bit of dat seasonin' gone. You saying all the words and intonations and usin' the right tenses and shit," I laugh and then turn my face into puppy eyes, "it's cuz you been up there for a while, and y'on think we important. I mean y'on even come visit us anymore."

Reader, you already know I gotta stir up some shit, but damn. I miss the old Marcus. Don't get me wrong, he was no different than this Marcus, but at least he ain't sound like a robot. His voice has always been deep and slightly "proper," but this is more cut, more enunciative, more community-outreach role model, more "you can make a difference in the Middle East, son" type of vibe, less Brooklyn. Back then, he could say fruity shit without it actually soundin' fruity, and I envied dat cuz I've always wanted to but he never did. Now, if he were it definitely would. On top of it all, he don't even text or chill or come through no more. As much as he hated it, he actually enjoyed bein' the voice of reason and the spectator to the wild shit me and Jordan would do in high school. He even—

I momentarily look at Marcus. Man, he ugly as fuck. Need to hook 'im up with Flaco o Pollo. Dat's my other love—I mean—barber, reader—anyways reader—over the years, he even started to open up a lil bit more. But after graduating, after being apart for so long and meeting up from time to time … now it's weird, cuz I know he's tryin' to do shit, but he makes me feel like a bitter girlfriend, always talkin' 'bout the lil things. Now I'm here askin' 'im why he don't take time out his day to be wit us. He became the hardest to contact, the hardest to link wit, and the hardest to talk to. He just became trapped in his head, undoin' the years of us gettin' closer to finally get to know a lil of what he was thinkin'. I kinda guessed witout seein' 'im dat he was gon' be different, but now I really know. Then again, we not the same either. We not the same kids we were three years ago. And I'on think dat's a problem, but change isn't always good when it comes at the detriment of your friends, and the people dat's always there for you.

"Yeah, my bad," he looks into the distance, his eyes guiltily fixated, "I just been having a lot on my plate and mind."

"Nigga took one philosophy and psychology class and think he Aristotle," Jordan jokes.

Reader, I'm tellin' you ... an education does wonders. I mean, no funny shit, CUNYs are dead responsible for the greatest upward mobility in the city. I'm surprised Jordan knows who Aristotle is. If you can teach 'im, we might not be so lost as people after all.

"Nah," I look at Jordan with approval, "he's def a Plato."

"What's the difference?" Jordan asks.

Sigh. Well, I mean ... you can't expect an education to be perfect. At least he tryin'.

"Plato thinks of the world as set in stone, while Aristotle saw more wiggle room in life," I dumb down the concept for Jordan to understand, "y'all not learnin' dat at Brooklyn College?"

"You ain't even dat much smarter than me."

"Marcus don't see shit past his own problems," I ignore Jordan and continue explainin', "he don't see past what's written in stone."

Marcus looks down at his watch and begins to rub the leather on it. The three of us become silent. I, for dramatic effect. Jordan cuz he's weirded out, and Marcus cuz damn, nigga ... I'm right. He's always been one to bitch and moan 'bout how shit is. I bet he said some dumb shit earlier 'bout how shit don't change, but at the same time not comin' to terms with the changes. Reader, tell me I'm right. Shiiet, I knew it, but I can't always be right. Sometimes, I gotta be funny. I reach into my bag, again fondlin' it like a titty, reach inside to the bottom and pull out a hat. I put it on my head and break the silence.

"You gotta see the chisel behind the stone, my brother," I point at my brain, emulatin' the best hotep voice I can muster, "*They* don't want you to know you're capable."

A SUS REUNION · 85

Marcus's guilty face dissipates as he shakes his head and smirks. He brings his hand up to his mouth hidin' his smile. "Bruh, you trippin'."

"I may trip, my brother, but I never fall." I look over to Jordan and back to Marcus. "But y'know what they say, the one who trips and does not fall, takes a step forward or sum like dat."

"Hmm, preach br—brother Abel," Jordan pushes to contain his laughter.

"I said," I put my hand on Marcus's shoulder and shout in his ear, "*my brother—*"

He slaps my hand off and moves his ear away from me as he looks around and apologizes to people now staring at us, "I'm sorry he's just a little differe—"

I put my hand back on his shoulder. "The one who trips and does not fall, takes a step forward."

"You a whole clown son," Jordan busts at the seams with laughter.

"You gotta come back and chill with the homies more," I point out to Marcus with my normal voice, "look at you, it hasn't been ten minutes in and you already cheesin'."

"Why you even have dat?" Jordan asks.

"I like to put it on cuz of dat show *Alke* … *Alk*-sum. The new African mythology show they started last year."

"Yeah, I know 'bout it."

"Dat shit got these young'uns gullible now."

"Nah, you wylin'," he says. "Niggas be in playgrounds and after-school programs with the kente cloth talkin' to kids? Wild."

"I'm a hotep at worst, not a Catholic priest. Ain't no diddling on this side."

86 · THE BOROUGHS

"You tweakin'," Jordan shakes his head, while smiling at a jogger as she passes by. Nothin' better than a piece a' ass to keep Jordan's attention. Reader, why are men so easy to understand. I shake my head in fake disapproval, as I look at the booty with 'im and smile.

"Y'know why she chose to meet here?" Jordan asks.

"Ionno brother," I sigh, "but she prolly on some dumb shit."

"Oh there's Alex," Marcus's face dies down back to normal and he shakes his head. He looks to the right, stands up, and waves his hand high, catching Alex's attention as she begins walking toward us.

CHAPTER 6

A RETROSPECTIVE WALK TO THE FUTURE

JORDAN
[In front of Delacorte Theatre, Central Park]
[Manhattan]
[12:18 p.m.]

"Y'know why she chose to meet here?" I ask. She better not have brought us here on no bullshit. If das the type of time she on, then I'mma be tight. Mostly cuz there's no reason to bring us along to those types of things. Just do what you have to do, do your little pictures or videos, and then call us after the fact so we can meet up and eat. I could be workin' right now, but also … this is nice. I'm glad we gon' hang out. Shit, I'm even glad Abel's here even if I can't stand 'im.

"I'on know brother," Abel sighs, "but she prolly on some dumb shit."

I look in Alex's direction, her big ass forehead boomin' past 'er curly hair. I always hated when she wears 'er hair up like that, you could always see dat big bulb from a mile away. At least 'er shit spotless, no acne. Maybe Abel's forehead braille jokes actually got to 'er back then. Cleaned up 'er shit real quick.

From a distance, she smiles widely, perkin' 'er nose up, and showcasin' pearly white teeth. As she walks closer, I see 'er distinctive curvy silhouette. Damn ... I see dat 'er forehead ain't the only thing big now. Shorty got more ass now than I remember. Her IG pics don't do 'er justice. I'm not gon' say anythin' tho, cuz I'm tryna be respectful and I know females ain't trynna hear dat. I'm sure Abel will say sum tho. Abel's never had a filter, and if there's sum dat hasn't changed after all these years and prolly never will, it's dat. The amount of times fights and arguments have broke out cuz of Abel's fuckery is tantamount to a gold Olympic medal. With a slick tongue like his ... no wonder he's a comedian. This entire day is just gon' be Abel plottin' and chatting up ways to make Alex mad.

"What's goodie Alexandria," Abel scans 'er up and down, head to toe, with a cheeky smile, "I see you been eatin' well."

"Aww, you and all the homeless guys are so sweet today," she says smiling.

"J. Cole back in town?" Abel shoots back with a smug face.

"Ugh. It's good to see y'all don't change," she says with a cold, stank face only Alex could muster. "Dogs."

"Woof," Abel mocks 'er.

"Y'all better not be catcalling women out here." She jabs 'er finger into Abel.

"Ay, y'all used to bully the ugly girls cuz they never got catcalled in high school," Abel quickly responds, "I ain't forget."

"Y'know I was about to say how much I've missed you but having you here now..." Alex rolls 'er eyes, collectin' and groupin' 'im together in bundled fingers, as if pinchin' salt in midair.

"Y'all? Whatchu mean y'all," I stand up and reach over to give 'er a hug, "I ain't say shit."

"So, you weren't checking me out?" she playfully asks and punches my chest lightly. She opens 'er arms and embraces me, swayin' me side to side. Damn, this is nice. She releases and holds me at arm's lengths.

"Of course I did…" I say admittedly. I know she been hittin' 'er lil gym. She been on dat grind. Her lil squat booty showin' out. I continue, "…respectfully tho."

"Aww, that makes it so much better." She winks at me then turns to Abel in disgust.

She looks at Marcus and then back at Abel with a face of realization. "Actually, where have you been? I saw you around midtown last week and was gonna say hi, but you looked like you were going somewhere quickly. I actually haven't seen you on campus since last semester."

Abel sucks his teeth, pursin' his lips together with his head leanin' back. "One, NYU don't got a campus and two, I'm taking a break from NYU's no-having-ass campus."

"What?" she looks at 'im suspiciously.

"Yeah, y'know the vibes. Fuck school. I got bored—"

"I—I can't deal with you," she dismisses Abel, hand viciously fannin' him away. She turns to Marcus, who has been patiently and quietly waitin' to be acknowledged. She daps 'im up and brings 'im in, squeezin' 'im into her. "I missed you so much, Marcus."

He smiles and steps back as he's released from the hug. "How've you been?"

"Oh so you want to know about me?" She leans back, actin' all surprised at his question. She clutches 'er non-existent necklace playfully. "You'd know if you answered my texts and didn't leave me on seen all the time."

Deadass tho. I be tryin' to link with 'im all the time and all I ever get is bein' left on read and gettin' sent straight to voicemail ... like damn what they got goin' on up there? A plantation? You can't take a day off to come visit? It don't even gotta be much. Just you and me chillin' at the dorm for some quality bro time would be fine.

"Hop off his dick. Dat man busy up there," Abel chimes. "He actually gotta study. He not goin' to bumass NYU, he goin' to Columbia—c-o-l-u-m-b-i-a. He trynna be a big steppa. Blow money on hoes and..."

Alex turns around and ignores Abel as he monologues and rambles behind her.

"So why are we here?" Marcus says, changin' the topic.

Alex takes 'er backpack off and places it right in front of 'er, supportin' its weight on the bench. She takes out a camera and shakes it, lettin' the red and black strap droop as she tightly holds the body of the bulky camera. Damn, dat camera look wild expensive to me.

"Better question," Abel smiles cheekily, "how you gon' invite us and then be late?"

"Deadass." I sit back down on the bench. Y'know for someone who sets up plans, she rarely ever gets there on time. How you gon' get ya ass handed to you by me and Abel. Only Caribbean folk here and we always make it on time. Caribbean folks will get to a function like two to three hours late, so technically we all early, but that only works if we *all* Caribbean. If we not ... then, well, shit. Shit is disastrous. Not to mention, I thought when we said we was gon' meet up, we was gon' go eat or some shit at We Are, or be on some Korean BBQ–type beat. Maybe some Jamaican food, but nah.

We out here in this bum ass park, for what? There ain't shit to do here. Fuck we gon' do here? What we gon' do? Set up a picnic? Blankets? Who brought food? I'm hungry as hell. This a whole dub and three-quarters.

"Okay, I'm late so—"

"So when we eatin'?" I interrupt 'er as Abel looks at me and chuckles.

"We just ate like an hour ago," Marcus says.

"Well, I'm hungry again."

"We can eat after…" She pauses and holds 'er camera up, signaling us to follow 'er as she starts walkin'. She continues, "Y'all just keep me company while I get these pictures for this project of mine."

Me and Abel look at each other and suck our teeths together in unison. Pause. I knew it. I knew we were gonna be here keepin' 'er company on some dumb shit. I knew it. The wild thing is we not even gon' help, she just wants people around 'er as she takes these pics. She always be in the group chat talkin' 'bout some "come to this march," "come to this meeting," "come to this event," "help me with this." Damn shorty, you don't got other friends? I be seein' 'em shits on IG when she post up all 'er videos and pics, but nun of us ever go. Fuck i'mma do at a rally? Get arrested? At an event? Meet 'er weird ass college friends? At a meetin'? Be the topic of conversation? Have 'em say sum stupid? Nah.

"So that's why we're here?" Marcus asks.

"Nah, c'mon, I'm not trynna do allat today," Abel says. "I really came here to chill."

"It's just gonna take a little bit and then we can go eat," Alex tries to convince us. "Seneca Village then eat. I'll even pay for you guys."

"I ain't lettin' no female pay for my shit," Abel comments.

A RETROSPECTIVE WALK TO THE FUTURE · 93

"Shit, I will," I say, "I'm on a different type of time. Das a free meal."

"Seneca Village?" Marcus questions as we start walkin' up through the track.

"Y'on know 'bout dat?" I ask. Sheesh. Here I thought Marcus was the smartest one of us all. Das some Marcus-type shit tho. He ain't the type to really pay attention to stuff like dat. He always had a disdain for things he never needed. History was one of those things. The past for 'im didn't exist, which never made any sense ... cuz ... the past is everythin'. Right as the present transitions into the past you actively alter the future. Every sentence and every word I breathe, speak, and think has led me to this very point in time. It defines where we are in the moment ... but of course ... it doesn't define where we go, and to Marcus, goin' wherever he wants to go is far more important than to look back to see where he came from.

"Nah." He extends his lower lip and shakes his head.

"Seneca Village was—"

"Basically," Abel chimes in, "Seneca Village was—"

Here we go.

"—a small town settlement dat existed here before the expansion of New York City up Manhattan. It—"

Alex jumps in, makin' it obvious by 'er tone dat she knows what Abel is doin', "It *was* a *settlement* started by freed slaves, one of the very first few safe havens for those who came up North to be free."

"That sounds pretty big? How come I never heard of it?" Marcus says.

"Cuz you never pay attention to shit like dat," I say.

"Deceased booty bro," Abel adds, "but to be fair tho, dat section of the course was non-existent."

"Yeah, and most people don't really know about it like dat," I say.

"Alright, but *why* are *we* here?" Marcus sighs, "And why couldn't we just meet there or after?"

"Cuz Alex annoying," Abel says.

"Because the entire area is kind of spread out and unrecognizable except for a few signs," Alex explains while ignorin' Abel. "Plus it was easier to just meet in front of the theatre."

"Hmm," Marcus groans.

I look at Marcus as he looks down at his watch. Damn, I get you ain't wanna be here, but man you could at least act like you do. It's not like time gonna go any faster.

"I also wanted to go to Summit Rock since it's the highest point and you can see the area where it used to be from there." Alex skips on the path, her camera swayin' back and forth with 'er cadence.

"Okay then," Marcus sighs.

I walk next to Alex as we weave past couples, families, strollers, and dog walkers. We walk straight until we hit the corner with a frank street vendor and then turn right on West Drive as we walk up the park. My eyes wander around from person to person, all either blank faced occupied on gettin' somewhere or calm ones layin' on blankets readin' under the shade. The streets is full of bikers, children playin' around, big and small booty women alike, and weirdly enough, a lot of joggin' old ladies. Ain't it a lil hot for dat? What if they have a heat stroke?

Walkin' next to me, Alex's ass jiggles slightly in cadence with 'er steps. Shit dummy fat, for real. I slow my steps, naturally startin' to get behind 'er ... until my back meets Abel's hand. He swings his arm forward and around my shoulder. Lookin' at me, he smiles from ear to ear, holdin' back the

A RETROSPECTIVE WALK TO THE FUTURE · 95

laughs of his cock-blockin' success. He walks us next to Alex, where she turns toward us with suspicion. Immediately, he changes his face to makin' the most nonchalant and dumbfounded face he could make, almost like someone whispered his name, but couldn't find who said it.

She gives a look of disapproval, her eyes zonin' Abel up and down from his fresh kicks to his fresh fade.

"We just happy to be here wit y'all, y'know?" Abel shakes me with his arm. "Ain't dat right, Jordan?"

I admit defeat, scoffin' Abel's hand off my shoulder, makin' it look like he was the one engagin' on some sus shit.

"Y'all are weird."

"Y'aLl ArE WeIrD," Abel mocks.

Alex takes the lead and walks forward and Abel joins 'er. A slight breeze blows past us as the tree rustles above us, some leaves fallin' as we walk up the path.

"It's not as hot as I thought it'd be," Abel says in the front.

"What are you talking about?" Alex fans 'er shirt. "This summer has been so fucking hot."

"It's only eighty-nine degrees out. It ain't even dat bad," he sucks his teeth, "y'all remember the week of July eleventh tho? Now *dat* was hot."

"*Yo*, the Wednesday of dat week, son...," I scream. "My socks were drenched when I got back home from workin' outside. I'm talkin' 'bout I wrung 'em shits."

"I know, I was outside too. Shit was one hundred and seven degrees out," Abel remarks. "Dat whole week was over one hundred degrees. I ain't never seen sum like dat in my life."

"Nah. Y'all different. I stayed inside that entire week," Alex chuckles.

"Yeah that day was actually unbearable," Marcus says. "My work building actually had a few power outages throughout the entire week."

"These politicians need to start taking climate change seriously." Alex shakes 'er head and looks back at us.

"Nah, let 'em warm it up. Fuck it up for everyone," Abel jokes. "Let humanity learn the hard way, since they wanna be pussy and not make some hard decisions."

Alex raises 'er eyebrows and wears a face of disapproval at Abel's joke, which he catches and continues to instigate.

"We not willin' to go into the homes of bankers, politicians, and the wealthy, and cuttin' some heads off," Abel continues, "I'm just sayin' … we prolly deserve our deaths by planetary oven."

"You talkin' mad reckless right now." I point at a pigeon walkin' near us. "Shush they listenin' right—"

"*Death to President Cockett,*" Abel says loudly at the pigeon.

The pigeon, startled, rapidly splats itself into a nearby tree in flight. It hits the ground, whirrin' its wings tryin' to fly again the entire way down. It stands up then skips and hops into the air, only to be grounded again by an unresponsive wing. The pigeon turns and stares at us, idly watching as we walk past, only to turn and walk toward some benches with nearby people.

"Wow," Marcus says blandly as the pigeon walks away.

"That's concerning," Alex says. "If you disappear at least we'll know why."

"Ayy, weirder shit has happened," Abel laughs as he swings his backpack over, slips his journal out and writes sum, immediately droppin' it back in. "Y'know what dat reminds me of … remember when the halal cart scandal happened?"

"Please stop," Marcus says immediately, forcin' down a smile.

"We really watched 'em do a public execution of a chicken—" Abel laughs loudly and uncontrollably, turnin' heads of everyone passin' down the drive.

"That was not funny," Alex says with a smile on 'er face, pushin' Abel as he stumbles slightly onto the grass, tryin' to get a hold of 'imself. She continues, "It was very traumatic. That's why so many people are vegan now."

"Shieet, not me," I laugh as Abel wheezily laughs and reaches over to daps me up.

"I don't even understand how it got to that point," Marcus says.

"Deadass. They ain't have to do allat," I say.

"Son…" Abel gasps for air as he moves to the side, lettin' a lady pass. He looks back. "Yo, all they had to say was they shit halal and dat they certified. Show some paperwork and they'd be all gucci, but nah."

The halal cart scandal happened two years ago, when there was rumors dat the meat used in a major halal cart in the city wasn't really … halal. Instead of just sayin' "nah our shit is halal," the owners dead just decided to kill a chicken in broad daylight … the halal way. Unfortunately, the chicken became agitated cuz there was mad heads there, and they missed cuttin' the artery properly. The chicken got loose and leaked blood on some of the people spectatin', and the rest is history. The halal cart scandal.

"Stop," Alex holds 'er laugh in, "people lost jobs and the halal trucks around the city shut down when people stopped going to them."

"They did a whole *60 Minutes* edition about it," Abel continues as he wipes the tears off his eyes.

"Alright relax, it's only a little funny." Alex fans Abel's cryin' eyes.

"That's a whole hour of my life I can't get back," Marcus shakes his head.

"Ayo, whoever shouted 'Allahu Akbar' when they was cuttin' the chicken's neck is a menace," Abel laughs.

"Please stop." Alex shakes 'er head in disapproval.

"Das a lil too much," I say, "you goin' too far."

"I wasn't even the one dat said it," Abel defends 'imself. "Jesus. This why comedy is dead."

"Y'know there's evidence actually that shows Amagone was the one that started that rumor," Alex says, "and they also helped the cart convince the city to let them do it."

"Damn hop off Amagone's dick." Abel wipes the sweat off his forehead. "What's next? They provided the chicken too?"

"I mean they did own the—"

"Amagone owns everythin' tho," I say.

Speakin' of the devil. In the distance, a bit before the arch, I see a rollin' street vendor cart across the street. Wearin' a white shirt and orange shorts, the vendor pushes 'er cart with a goat's face on it as she walks opposite of us across the street. She stops and serves what seems to be a joggin' duo competin' to see who gets there first. The shorty with the sports bra gets there first, dramatically stickin' out 'er tongue. I hate that shit. I'on really understand why females do dat. Like damn put dat shit back in your mouth. The second jogger stops right behind the winner, flailin' 'er dead arms from side to side, sweat brimmin' off 'er fingertips.

"Aye, I got an employee discount." I point at the ice cream vendor. "Y'all want some goat ice cream?"

"Hell no," Alex immediately rejects my offer.

"Ayooo, don't they be milkin' dat shit down in Queens?" Abel perks up with a face of disgust which then turns complacent. "I'll try one if it's free."

"Marcus?"

"I mean," he thinks hesitantly, "why not?"

We all start crossin' the street toward the street vendor, but stop at the cluckin' of hoofs resonatin' behind us. We stare as two police officers on horses pass by from behind, one of 'em tippin' his hat toward us.

"Howdy massa," Abel joins his hands together as if in bondage as the police officers pass, their expressionless faces goin' sour.

"This—" I look at Abel. "You doin' too much today bro. You trynna get a mural repainted or sum?"

He watches as the horses continue to walk on by. "They're police horse riders. When was the last time you ever seen 'em do shit?"

"Never," Alex says.

"Exactly. Waste of my tax dollars." He shrugs his shoulders. "So I might as well make fun of 'em."

We continue to cross the street toward the goat ice cream. The lady smiles at us and opens the metal lids of each flavor, showcasin' white, orange, and red velvety ice cream in the cans.

"Wow," Alex laughs defeatedly, "that's actually funny."

"Coconut, Mango, and Cherry," I say defeatedly. The coco-mango-cherry folks of New York are no more. The only thing remainin' was these joints, the ones that Amagone repurposed when the city cracked down heavy on street vendors. They came for coco-mango-cherry folks, then the churro ladies. The mango ladies were the last to go and the most heartbreakin' of all. Shit was devastatin'. The only ripe mangoes in the city … gone.

"Let me get mango," Marcus sighs and looks at his watch.

"Yeah, let me get one of those too," Abel says.

"Three mangoes, please." I smile at the lady as she signals to the interface chargin' me a total of $6.75. I enter my code: "GIGWORKERS50" for half off, tip 'er fifteen percent, and tap my card on the interface. A thank you notification pops up as she scoops three mini-cup sized mango ice creams. She hands 'em to us, forcefully smiles, waves, and carries on as we walk away.

"You guys are disgusting," Alex says with a nauseated face as we eat our ice cream.

"Shorty got poor customer service skills man," Abel says as he slurps his ice cream very obviously sexually. "She ain't even say hi or bye or nothin'."

"Neither did you, clown," Alex says.

"Jordan, did you tip 'er?" Abel asks.

"Yeah."

"Disgraceful."

"You're a horrible person," Alex says. "It's bad enough she gets paid minimum wage."

"Damn, this is better than the OGs," Abel says, lickin' the ice cream drippin' from the brim of the cup. Gay ass nigga.

"I wouldn't say allat," I say.

"Nah, these are better," Marcus agrees with Abel.

"Despicable," Alex huffs as she walks in front of us. She looks up into the sky, left arm by 'er waist, her right fannin' 'er shirt to cool off. Her camera jangles, bouncin' off 'er hips. She looks at us doggin' the ice cream and says, "I miss the mango ladies."

"Amagone needs to do a mango service, so we can get the ripe mangoes back," Abel says.

"They probably will the way things are going," Alex asserts. "I'm telling you, they're a problem."

"As long as my packages get to me on time and I got mangoes…" Abel instigates. "I don't mind 'em at all. They could keep mistreatin' their workers."

"How does that even work?" Marcus changes the subject quickly, knowin' where the conversation could lead.

"What?" I say, catchin' his drift. "The cart?"

"How do you work the cart?" Marcus asks.

"It's like Uber or Lyft. You pick up the cart and make sales," I say. "You work whatever hours you wanna work and then you take 'em back to the storage units around the city, where they refill 'em."

"Wow, they really gentrified and ride-shared the coco-mango-cherry," Abel says. "At least it tastes better."

And dat they did. They gentrified the shit outta it. Just like everythin' else. We walk in silence while eatin' our ice cream. Marcus and I fall to the back as Alex takes lead, Abel inchin' his way next to 'er as we walk to the site—Seneca Village. I wonder if any of the people in the park know about it. The history of this park or any of the people dat came before 'em. Would the future remember us in dat way or would they just forget us? I mean, it's not like we bein' remembered now … so it wouldn't surprise me if we ain't then. I mean das how it be tho. I mean there were people here before and no one really remembers 'em. And even before those people, there were people here, and we don't remember 'em either.

"Jordan?" Marcus says.

"What?"

"Your ice cream's dripping from your hand."

"Aw fuck." I wave it in front of me away from my shirt.

"You okay, man?"

"Yeah, why?"

"You just looked off for a second," Marcus says, "this morning too."

"Dat was cuz of your crazy aunt," I shake my head, "wild."

"I'm talking about after the bodega ... at the park."

"Hmm," I pause, "Nah I just kinda been thinkin' 'bout some shit."

"Hmmm," Marcus says, "What are you thinking about?"

...

"You think these people know dat there were folks here before 'em?"

"I think I'm pretty smart," Marcus says confidently. "If I didn't know, it wouldn't surprise me if they didn't either."

"Yeah," I look at 'im sideways and shake my head. "You think they care?"

"I mean if it was a long ass time ago, why would anyone?"

"Yeah, I guess you right 'bout dat," I say. "You'd think they'd care if it was happenin' right in front of 'em?"

"Man, what are you saying?"

"Nothin'."

Marcus wouldn't understand either way. He clearly doesn't care what happens back home. His mind has always been set on leavin' it, never really improvin' it or just trynna stay there, and in a way I understand. One way or another, you're either meant to feel like you can't move forward without leavin', but shit is changin' so much and so fast dat you don't really fit in there either. You just in a limbo state trynna find yourself. Shit just seems hopeless sometimes.

"They don't," Alex shouts back as she continues walkin'.

"What?"

A RETROSPECTIVE WALK TO THE FUTURE · 103

"They don't care about gentrification," Alex says as she turns 'er head while still walkin' forward. "Well, most of them aren't even aware of it."

"Hey hey, don't just throw the G-word around," Abel adds jokingly, "shit's offensive."

"What is your project even about, Alex?" I ask.

"The G-word." She looks at Abel with a smile.

"Gay," Abel says smilin' back at her.

She sighs and points ahead as we walk to a fork, where West Drive diverges to two lanes, one going deeper into the park and the other continuin' straight. On the sidewalk, we turn left onto a steep, windin', snake-like trail, which opens onto a vast clearin' surrounded by trees, the only gap showcasin' the NYC buildings. She points at the clearin'. "This is it. This is where Seneca Village started, Summit Rock."

"So people used to live here?" Marcus asks.

"Yup," Alex says.

"I never knew there were hilly parts like this in the park," I say.

"Y'know Manhattan actually means lands of rocky hills, or sum like dat," Abel says. "The Lenape people called it dat and when the Europeans came, they just co-opted it."

"Oh wow," Alex says surprised, lookin' at me and Marcus, "Abel actually has something smart and inoffensive to say."

Abel looks at 'er with a dim smile. "I have a comedy show tonight. You're all comin'. It's nonnegotiable."

"I don't know about th—"

"You're comin' and dat's it," Abel interrupts Marcus, who just sighs complacently knowin' he's goin' to end up comin' anyways.

"I haven't been to a comedy show in years," Alex says.

"Okay then, take your lil pics, let's eat, play some pool and then it's my time," Abel says slappin' his hands. "Go ahead. Take your pics."

"What this gotta do with your project?" I ask.

"Umm, hello? Are you dumb?" Alex puts a stank face on as she snaps pictures. "People being pushed out. Does that sound like anything to you?"

"She's trynna make connections to changes in the city," Marcus clarifies as she nods in agreement.

"Ahh this your lil IG project, huh?" Abel questions.

"I get your point, but what's the difference between what's happening back then to just moving out the neighborhood? The Italians and the Irish?"

"I mean you can't equate bein' pushed out to being able to stay but leavin' cuz you don't wanna be next to negros and spics," Abel says with a smirk as he turns to Alex, his hands in the air. "Those are their words not mine."

Alex sighs.

"Fair enough," Marcus says as he sits down on a nearby rock-sculpted seat, fidgetin' with his watch.

I sit on the inside of a Y-shaped tree as Alex continues to take pictures of the surroundin' area. Abel goes by the edge of the hill, lookin' out onto Central Park West, only stopped by the sudden drop into leaves, foliage, and rocks. He lets out an evil chuckle as he swings his backpack in front of 'im. He brings out his journal and starts to write in it like crazy.

CHAPTER 7

THE PINK HATS ARE EVERYWHERE

ALEX
[Summit Rock, Central Park]
[Manhattan]
[12:47 p.m.]

"Move for a bit." I signal Jordan to move as I take a picture of a tree in the middle of the opening. This area is actually really nice. There's a spacious, grassy, middle area surrounded by sun-covering trees. It's definitely perfect for picnics. Aside from the buildings in the background, this is so filled with green, you wouldn't even think you were in the city. Of course, the polluted air and the traffic noise would be a dead giveaway. I fan my shirt and walk a bit down the road where we came from and snap more pictures as we come into the clearing from a downward angle. Across the clearing, I watch as Marcus and Jordan sit on a rock together talking about his watch, while Abel overlooks what's happening on the street. I walk toward him, standing right next to him as I watch him write something down in his joke book.

Down on the street, there are small groups of women passing through, their presence pushing joggers and onlookers to the side as an inundation of pink enters the park. Oh yeah … oh no. This is *that* women's march. They had broken off from the larger protests in Central Park West, swarming West Drive and West 85th within the park, and although the legality of whether they could protest within it was in question, of course, the NYPD stationed officers across the street do absolutely nothing. I thought they wouldn't take this route and stay closer to midtown, but no.

I take one last picture of the area, sling my camera over my body by its strap, and signal the guys to follow me. Abel watches the crowd attentively as he keeps writing down things in his joke book. I hate that. He brings it everywhere he goes, no matter the occasion. He's maniacal like that. Abel is the type to let you know through a *seemingly* normal conversation that *that* is his joke book, and once he has established that, he just continuously opens it mid-conversation and writes something in it. He once made my friend feel very self-conscious while having lunch by continuously writing in it every time she spoke. She left early that day back to her apartment. I felt so bad.

The thing is … I glanced at it at the time, and all he had written in capital letters was: "BIG forehead in a mirror house," "Abortions," and "GREAT WALL OF CHINA." That's it. I don't even know if those are just coded little messages or if he's just fucking around or if people stressing trying to get the joke *is* the actual joke. I—I don't know. That's the thing about him, you don't know if he's being serious or not, or even if the joke book itself is just part of a bigger joke.

Not to say that he's not writing about people themselves or that he doesn't write actual notes. There's no way he'd put this much effort into something like this … right? I mean, not that it matters anyways. He writes in it and that bothers me. The way he's laughing right now … I can only imagine the crude and disgusting things he's writing down.

"You got the pictures you needed?" Marcus asks, fidgeting with the straps of his backpack, adjusting the slings from really baggy to really tight. He's clearly bored by it all. Does he even want to hang out with us? It took me begging him all summer and free time in everyone's schedule—circumstances he couldn't refuse without making it painfully obvious he didn't want to spend time with us. Ultimately, the person that got him to come out was none other than Abel. All Abel had to say was "You gon' come?" And he did.

"Yeah, I'm almost done."

"So how's this even gon' work?" Jordan asks.

"I've taken pictures of everything around the city." I grab my camera strapped around me. "I got pictures posted from all over the boroughs to bring some awareness to the problem."

"Damn, you went all the way to Staten Island too?"

"Umm…," I've lived here my whole life and not once have I gone over there, "no."

"Naturally," Abel chimes in, his joke book closed and dangling from his pointer finger in between the pages. "A wise man once said, 'Fuck errbody in Staten Island, but the Wu-Tang Clan.'"

"C'mon now, my man Messiah is from there," Jordan comes to the defense.

"Well, you better be Pontius Pilate and wash ya hands," Abel returns rapidly, almost like he has it ready before you've even finished what you're saying. He turns to me, pointing at my camera. "You got 'em?"

"Yeah. Now, I just need some near the signs over there." I gesture toward the direction of the main site, down the hill and up the park. We walk down the hill and out into the open past the thick tree area. The pink pussy hats—oh no. We walk down the hill onto the pavement road leading to the actual Seneca Village site. The village was sprawled around the area. It was sizable and once had many homes and families, but now, all of that is gone. The village site looks no different from any other part of the park. In fact, other than some of the signs, and the big protruding rocks present around the area, there is no visible testimony of there ever being a town here; of course, that in itself is a testament of how wild the eminent push was.

"So, they pushed everyone out, created the park, and where did the people go? Marcus asks.

"They just scattered, I think," Abel says.

"Damn, imagine if they hadn't pushed out the neighborhood—," Jordan chimes, "just built the park around it. This would def be the spot."

"Who says they wouldn't have eventually taken dat too?" Abel says. "Look at Harlem."

"They'd do it still and all for the sake of vanity," I continue. And that it was. It didn't matter the signs erected surrounding the area, there was no level of respect for it. It was the bare minimum the city or anyone could do. Around the site were people on their blankets enjoying picnics, sunbathing, and playing soccer, probably not fully realizing the importance of it all. That there were people here who were pushed out, generations later to be forgotten, or just a niche little fact you tell at a cocktail party to impress your bubble-sequestered friends in the Upper West Side.

We continue to walk on the path toward the main site, the surrounding green space of the park sprinkled with pink hats, some of them dispersing from the break off group and sitting on the grass.

"What's good with the pink pussy hats?" Jordan laughs, catching the attention of several of their wearers, who promptly scowl at the comment.

"*Deadass*," Abel says, raising his voice slightly louder. "*Why's there mad pink pussies around here ... and I'm not talkin' 'bout the hats.*"

"Please stop," Marcus and I say in unison.

I swear, Abel is so immature and always looking for trouble.

It's always some unnecessary stupidity with him. Back in high school, his aunt had two miscarriages back-to-back. She painfully addressed the news to the family, to which he degenerately responded by asking whether a miscarriage was "one of those new genders or sum." The second time around, upon hearing the news, he responded with "damn that's crazy ... you strong tho." After two miscarriages and a baby, there was no surprise when she came out as an avid pro-life supporter. Knowing this, Abel spent nearly one hundred dollars to send her a custom baby onesie with the words "pro-choice" written in the front and "I support her right to murder a clump of cells" on the back. All, he claims, to lighten the mood, but anyone who knows him knows well that there's nothing in his brain other than chaos and trouble. Some of it is funny though ... like that one time he plastered NYC Pride stickers in the church seating minutes before the start of mass. But this—

Why is Marcus holding his mouth shut? Marcus comes up from holding his mouth with a smirk, shaking his head. He taps on Abel's shoulder, prompting him to turn toward Marcus to see his shaking head in disapproval, but his smirk, alongside the gesture does nothing but encourage him further.

"Oh nah, chill," Jordan says with a playful smile on his face, nodding his head, urging him on. I look at him square, shifting his smile and nod to a serious face of disapproval as he shakes his head toward Abel's shenanigans.

"You right." Abel simmers his voice down to a whisper. "Lemme stop. I'll stop…"

…

Oh no—

"Yo Alex, my female, vagina-carryin' friend, can you inform me of what is happenin' here today?"

"Abel. Shut. Up."

His comment brings about further head turns and scowls from the groups surrounding us. He knows what is happening. Clearly, it's a women's march and hopefully he doesn't find out why it's happening. It's just going to light him up.

"Isn't the Women's March usually in the beginnin' of the year?" Jordan adds, trying to both innocently answer Abel's question and inquire more about the reason as to why there's one now in August.

"Yes, but I don't know—"

"Sis. Excuse me, sis." A pink hat approaches us from behind, another following close behind her. You could see behind them the group of women who were sitting in the green space, looking in our direction. I side-eye Abel. See what you did? I look back to Marcus and Jordan, and see

Abel's face light up, contrasted by Marcus's and Jordan's slightly annoyed faces.

"Oh." I am taken aback a bit. Abel holds his smile tightly to his face, lowering his voice and whispering to Jordan and Marcus behind me.

"Hi sis," her bubbly—

"*Sis?* Shorty, how you gon' call Alex *sis?*" Abel whispers behind me to the guys.

—personality shows through her voice. Wearing a white tee with no bra, big hoop earrings, mom jeans, and white shoes, she jangles—

"Ayo watch. Watch. Watch."

"Nah, chill." Jordan tries to calm Abel.

—her bracelets around, flamboyantly waving her hands so as to showcase her nails, "You should really join the march with us. Women's rights. *Period.*"

She pronounces the *d* in period like a *t*, in a laughably exaggerated manner.

Abel's face freezes in place, his entire body slightly vibrating as he contains his laughter. Jordan, holding Abel's shoulder, turns around facing back toward the summit, clearly ready to burst through the seams with laughter. Marcus, wearing a nonchalant smile, as if he's too cool to care, looks away and beyond, to the space behind the girls.

"Ah, I would," I unsling my camera from my shoulders and hold it in my hand, "but I'm currently working on a project ri—"

"Oh, what's it about?"

"It's about Seneca Village, a majority Black settlement that was here prior to the creation of the park," I explain. "It was one of the few places where free slaves could come and have a free life, and even have interracial marriages. It was a community open for all—"

"Oh, that's a nice ... little project you got there," the blonde girl interrupts, "we could use a camera to take pictures of us actually."

"*Little?*"

"Did you say interracial?" the brunette one comments, her bracelets moving slightly on—

"Ayo why shorty got a black spade tattoo?"

—her wrist—oh wait, Abel's right.

"Shorty dead trynna disappoint her pops, bro," Abel whispers.

"Please stop," Marcus whispers back to him.

I glance at the brunette girl's wrist as she adjusts her wide black bracelets around it, hiding her tattoo.

"Damn Jordan, I think she'd love you bro."

"You need to stop," Marcus chimes in chuckling.

"Jordan, I know you like being on a leash."

The boys bust out the seams, hollering and howling, slightly walking away from the group to laugh at Abel's jokes. Abel, staying strong in his conviction, holds in his laugh and joins me, looking back and forth between them embarrassed. Lucky for them and me, they didn't hear anything. That's sexual harassment.

"I'm so sorry," I say, shaking my head, "they're just ... men."

"Oh, don't worry," the blonde one says, "*we* underst—"

"Excuse me. Oh sorry for manterrupting. I know, I'm ... a man." Abel comes in playfully, making a disgusted denigrating himself, with his joke book open and pen in hand. "May I, a lowly man, ask what y'all marchin' for? They acting up over in Hollywood again?"

The main one, rightfully sensing Abel's bad faith, folds her arms and forcefully says, "We march against the patriarchy, we march against being belittled, objectified—"

Abel and I look at the brunette and smile subtly. She flinches and covers her wrist with her hand. He winks at her, not wasting time to capitalize on the moment.

"—but today, we're here because of the hysterectomies being performed on little girls at the border. It is so unfair that it's happening to those girls, while they're leaving the boys alone."

"Well, I think it's a travesty but—"

"Also," she interrupts me, "our president really said that there shouldn't be female guards. How are you a woman and not supporting other women that want to work in the system?"

"There's definitely nuance there—"

"And isn't it weird that she nearly everyone she appointed in her cabinet is male," she interrupts again.

Shit. Here we go. This is why I didn't want Abel to know.

"Hysterectomies?" Abel focuses on the first point.

He knows what those are.

"It's the mutilation of—"

"Nah shorty, I know what it is," Abel clarifies, writing down something in his book. I sway my body slightly and try to get a peek at his book. He immediately moves his journal, only letting me glimpse at one word: "Bucket." The guys had come back from their dispersed laugh session, Marcus laughing alongside Jordan. Well at least Marcus is having fun. Abel continues, "So y'all out here cuz of dat huh?"

"Yeah, we are," the main one reassures him as the brunette looks deeply at Jordan.

Here it goes.

THE PINK HATS ARE EVERYWHERE · 115

"Well. I think it's very admirable you guys are fightin' for the right things," he says in what seems a genuine tone, but I've known him for years—enough to know that with that smug face, there's nothing short to his words than passive aggressiveness reeking of sarcasm.

I wait for him to continue as the main and the support purse their lips forward nodding their heads, unconvinced of his support. He doesn't. I stare as they both look at each other for a little while until Abel closes his book, turns to face the guys, and walks away from the duo. That's it? I look back at Abel as he waves at them and walks away. You have a perfect opportunity to shred into something so deliberately stupid, and you don't? What? Maybe he's a little sick?

"Abel?" I ask as he smiles, opens his journal again, shakes his head, scribbles something in it, and shuts it.

"It was real nice talkin' to you gorgeous activist broads," Abel says as he faces back, waves, then signals toward the direction of the main site, "but we got this lil project of hers to finish. Thank you tho. It was really educational."

We walk past the girls as we continue our way to the plaque that signifies the middle of the site. I look back to see the blonde one's confused face as the brunette looks at the guys attentively. Oh wow. There's a lot there to unpack. I turn around to see Abel's smiling face and tell him, "I'm proud of you for not saying anything."

"You good? Is the heat gettin' to you, bro?" Jordan seems worried and confused as he asks, "You alright? Like for real, for real?"

"What you want me to say?" Abel smiles. "I'm a changed man."

"Oh c'mon," Marcus chimes in, surprisingly entertaining the conversation. "You always have something to say."

"Some things just speak for themselves man." Abel sways his joke book around. "I ain't gotta say shit."

"Right," I say. "Y'know, for a second there, I thought you really were just speechless."

Abel walks in silence with a shaking, smug face. We walk a couple steps until we all realize that the impossible has happened. We all look at each other and say in unison, "*Naw*."

Abel sucks his teeth.

"Wow," Marcus says with an *actual* smile on his face, "I'm not gonna lie. This might be the reason I'm actually glad I came today."

"Ight, it's not even that serious." Abel fans his hands down.

"Fuck you mean not serious?" Jordan wraps his arms around Abel and snaps a selfie. "This might be a first."

"Bruh, how you gon' respond to dat?" Abel shoots back, scoffing Jordan's arm off. "Shorty really said that shit with a straight face. No jokes. No sarcasm. No introspection. No nothin'. Just vibes. Dumb bitch vibes."

We all laugh together as he continues on.

"She just … no education, no literature, just Instagram infographic posts."

"Hey, not everyone has the education or resources to understand some of the literature," I say, "they're helpful sometimes."

"Y'all underestimate people too much," he says. "Jordan can understand it, why can't they?"

"Ayo, suck my dick."

"Ask shorty over there," Abel retorts quickly. "You saw how she was looking at you?"

"Yeah," Jordan says proudly, "you can still suck my dick tho."

THE PINK HATS ARE EVERYWHERE · 117

"Aye, aye. Be careful, we standin' on sacred grounds," Abel jokes as he walks ahead and touches the Seneca Village plaque.

I grab my dangling camera and point it at the plaque, framing the dirty and scratched board in a way where the pink hats wouldn't be visible. Or maybe they should? Seems ironic that the very essence of resistance is now so corporative, so aesthetically pleasing, marketized and commodified to us all. I mean … how much were those hats? And who's selling them? Not that it matters, really. The Capitalist Gods have already co-opted all of it anyways.

"Yo, when you think about it," Abel says pensively as he looks at me, "all the shit you doin' right now is pointless."

"Facts," Jordan says. "You should've done this on your doley, without us. I was just trynna chill and eat."

"What?" I say as I decide to take the picture of the plaque and the park. If anything I can always just do some photoshop and delete the pink hats.

"Don't you think people gon' bastardize what you're doin' with all this?" Abel says.

"Well…"

"No, seriously," Abel interrupts, "You're in activist circles. You know. It happens with police brutality every summer, especially this summer. Happens with Pride every June. I mean, we just passed a group of pink hats."

"Who sells those?" Marcus wispily asks.

"I mean with that mentality, you wouldn't do anything." I purse my lips forward and shrug my shoulders. "You wouldn't fight for anything."

"If shit don't change and people just do this shit for the gram or whatever, then what's the point tho?" Abel asks rhetorically. "You wastin' time and energy."

"My project coalition has brought so many people around the city together," I say. "We share stories about how thing are changing and how hard life is in the city due to gentrification. Isn't the awareness important?"

"I give it a couple more weeks before some meathead misuses it." Abel sneezes into the air—ew—and sniffs. "In a couple months it's just gon' be one of those hashtags that cafés write on they lil chalkboards outside and you want us to waste our time on dat? Issa dub."

"Is that why y'all ain't come to any of my events in the summer? You think it's stupid?"

They all show their teeth and suck in air and turn their heads away from me.

"Why didn't you guys come to my events throughout the summer?" I push. "I worked really hard on them."

"You said it, not me," Abel says rapidly.

"Alex, I care about you, but I honestly don't think those events really help," Jordan says, clearly picking up slack for Abel. "I just feel like we talk a whole lot and shit never gets done. It's tirin' sometimes."

"But—"

"Plus," Jordan interrupts me, "why I gotta march with people that say I matter till the music a lil too loud?"

"Damn," Abel says as he opens his joke book and begins to scribble. Without looking up, he continues, "Shorty really thinks she can fight the system and corporations."

I sigh deeply, moving some of my hair out of my face behind my ears. I look at Marcus, shaking his head and looking down at his watch, avoiding eye contact so as to not answer the question. He looks up slightly and we lock eyes. Not being able to get away from me anymore, I grill him further until he breaks.

"I think it's nice that you fight for what you believe in," Marcus tiptoes around the issue. "I'd go but I have work and school."

"Don't lie to 'er, bro," Abel says looking at Marcus and grasping his shoulder tightly. "You also a double major and she's a film student."

"You're a film student too, you clown," I say defensively.

"Not anymore."

"You guys really don't care at all?"

"Shit," Jordan sighs. "I care … a lot, but I gotta take care of me and my mental, my mātha, y'feel me?"

"True, plus … me no Black, me Dominican," Abel jokes in a Spanish accent as he taps his chest, his expression bringing him to laughter. He clears his throat and continues, "I found out I was Black when I was sixteen. One day, I was confused why the NYPD was always on my dick, and now you want me to start marchin'?"

They all laugh in unison, Marcus the only one decent enough to turn his head. I grab my camera tightly, scoff, turn around, and keep taking pictures.

I get where they're coming from, but what's the alternative? Do nothing? What do you do when something happens in your city? In your community? It's a shame they feel that way about it. Movements aren't perfect, they take time and dedication to build. You gotta stay positive in the face of adversity and no matter how hard it is, you still gotta move forward, mobilize some people, and go out and do the necessary work. We always wish that there are people that do right by us, but maybe we should just do right by ourselves. We should advocate for ourselves. I don't know. Yeah there are people that use this for their personal image, but that doesn't take away from the movement itself.

In the distance, a pink hatter hails a walking man with a baby harness. I watch as she motions to her phone and then signals to her friends. Her friends immediately position themselves together so that their faces and arms make the shape of a vagina, leaving the top empty. I'm assuming that's for the other one. The man stares at them bewildered and hesitantly grabs the phone, waits for her to get in position at the very top, and takes the picture. Ugh.

I look at Abel, Jordan, and Marcus moping around behind me, overlooking the city skyline and talking about anime. I look down at my camera and see all the pictures I captured, pink hats littered throughout every single one of them. I sigh. This'll do, I guess.

"Let's just go eat," I say.

CHAPTER 8

A COMIC'S THESIS

MARCUS
[Korean BBQ Restaurant]
[Manhattan]
[2:48 p.m.]

"Nah, you can't tell me nothin' 'bout dat *Piece*," Jordan says as he stuffs his face with meat.

"Bro, you gon' tell me *One Piece* is not dragged out?" Abel sits forward.

"Nah, the story and the world buildin' is crazy," Jordan says, with a mouthful, in defense of his favorite childhood manga. "Oda is goated in my eyes."

"Bro, dat shit's played out."

"Nah—"

"People were born, went to school, met the love of their life, and probably have kids now," Alex interjects, "and it's still not done. I hate to agree with Abel, but it's dragged out a bit."

"Wooooww," Jordan exclaims.

"*Thank you*," Abel shouts as he looks down at his phone and taps it vigorously. "Shit came out in 1999. Bro, it's 2027."

"Get away from me." Jordan scoots farther into the booth as Alex attempts to soften her betrayal by laying her head on his shoulder. "I gotta mow the lawn. Snakes are everywhere nowadays."

"Didn't Oda, the creator, say two years ago that he was retiring," I add.

"Yeah—" Alex begins to say.

"He's been sayin' dat since 2024 when the Straw Hats found the treasure—" Abel says to me, and then turning to Jordan, "how it should have fuckin' ended."

"We wouldn't have gotten some of the coolest fights of the whole franchise then," Jordan says, "this current arc is the best one they've had on the show."

"No, it—" Alex scrunches her face in disbelief before putting soy sauce soaked meat in her mouth.

"You smokin' wild dick." Abel slams his fist on the table with every word he says. "This arc is better than Marineford and Wano?"

"Jordan, just admit that it's played out," I say.

"When was the last time you even read the manga?" Jordan asks me.

"Honestly," I say, "two years ago."

"Oh, so you don't even know what we talkin' 'bout," Abel says.

"Exactly." Jordan puts his arms to the air.

"If Oda keeps writing like this he might sully his legacy and the legacy of *One Piece*," Alex adds, licking the BBQ sauce off her chopsticks.

"True," Abel says.

"Wow," Jordan sits back on his chair. "Y'all gon' disrespect Oda's genius like dat."

"He disrespectin' 'imself," Abel says. "Just end the shit and live your life."

"He has to be a masochist," Alex adds. "Working those long hours and—"

I look down at my watch.

[Billiards Club]
[Manhattan]
[4:26 p.m.]

I look up from my watch.

Clack.

The white cue ball hits the last stripe ball as it gracefully rolls into the corner pocket. Alex flexes a bit by winking at Jordan and me. Unfortunately, I'm horrible at pool.

"Damn, I ain't know she had it like dat," Jordan says.

"Why you think I put dibs on 'er?" Abel says. "I'm so trash dat I'm practically a handicap."

Abel gets closer to the table, smiles at Alex, and—without breaking eye contact—forcefully hits the white ball, missing the black eight ball by a huge margin and sinking the cue into the table pocket.

He stands up straight, sighs dramatically, and shrugs his shoulders. "Oops."

"Dickhead," she says.

"Why?" Jordan and I say in unison. Jordan gets closer to the table.

"Why?" I say to him. "What do you gain? Just win so we can start the next game."

"I'm helping y'all," Abel says, and then whispers to me, "but more specifically, I'm helping out Jordan."

"Why?" I instinctively whisper too.

A COMIC'S THESIS · 125

"Look," Abel points at Jordan.

Jordan is extremely good at pool for some reason. Clearly not as good as Alex who is down to the last ball, but good enough to where she definitely feels the pressure. I mean, he's basically carried me throughout the two games we've just played. Jordan picks up the white ball from the ball opening and plops it down on the table. He gets down to the table's level and gauges the angles, checking to see what pocket of the table he can easily sink the ball to. He moves the white ball again and readies his pool stick. Immediately, Alex bends herself right next to Jordan, her elbows positioned on the table almost cat-like as she rests her chin on her hands. She leans her face into his ears.

"Miss," she whispers into his ear.

Jordan hits the white cue ball and it propels to a red solid ball that finds itself swiftly in the side pocket of the table. He stands up and smiles at her. He rubs the chalk on the tip of the pool stick almost sensually. She shakes her head, her face a mix of bewilderment and laughter.

"See," Abel whispers at me, then with his normal voice, he sucks his teeth and addresses the other two with, "Ay I don't mind bein' the cameraman."

"You're disgusting." Alex smiles cordially.

"Dat's gon' be a short video and the easiest fifty bucks I've ever made," Abel says.

"You'd take such a low rate?" I scrunch my face in question.

"If I get to see Jordan's weak ass stroke." Abel starts arrhythmically humping the pool table. "Yeah."

"Ew, nigga you gay," Jordan says to Alex's dismay as he sucks his teeth, ready for her lecture.

"We were doing so well today with *not* saying that word," Alex sighs disappointedly, massaging her forehead. She turns to Abel, "It is a little sus though."

I shake my head as all three of them ensue laughing.

I look down at my watch.

[Outside a Gelato Shop]
[Manhattan]
[6:36 p.m.]

I look up from my watch to a busy street. I lean back on the store glass front as people pass by laughing and holding hands. Cupping my hands around my paper cup, I look at my butter pecan gelato, the plastic spoon dug deep into the mound.

"Yo—good?" Abel bumps his shoulder into mine.

"Hmm," I say looking at him then back down to my gelato, "I haven't tasted it yet."

"I asked if *you* good, not the ice cream," Abel clarifies looking at my untouched gelato. "You better eat it all. I paid for dat expensive ass ice cream."

"It's gelato," I correct him.

"It's expensive," he says back, "dat's what it is."

"Yeah," I bring a scoop up to my mouth, "thank you."

It's good.

"But we only go out once in a while, so it's fine," he justifies.

"Hmm," I nod.

"You been quiet since we left the pool spot," Abel says as he scoops strawberry gelato into his mouth and looks down, "fuck dat's some good shit."

"I'm just here man." I scoop some more of the gelato up and put it in my mouth. Damn, that's actually really good.

"You havin' fun at least?" he asks.

"Yeah," I nod as I twirl the gelato in my mouth with my tongue. It has been a decent enough day. I saw Abel be speechless. We ate some really good meat. This gelato is actually not that bad either. It's better than the mango ice cream we had earlier.

"Dat's why you gotta chill with us more." He smiles at me.

"Yeah, I just got a lot on my mind," I say.

"Ay gang, if you ever need to talk…" Abel shrugs, hands in front of him, pointing at himself.

"You're just gonna laugh and joke the entire time," I say. Abel has always been a good friend, someone you can rely on. Unfortunately, he often can't take anything seriously.

"True," he smiles. "You glad you came tho?"

"Yeah."

"If you havin' fun tho then dat's all dat matters." He smiles as he turns his head over to Alex and Jordan, walking toward us from a nearby sweets shop, cupcakes in hand.

"I can't believe this," Alex says.

"What?" Abel asks.

"He—"

"Nah bro don't listen to 'er," Jordan says. "She actin' like I'm the crazy one."

"They offer a frosting flavor called 'manly strawberry,'" she explains. "It's virtually the same as normal strawberry and he paid an extra dollar for the manly one."

"Cuz I'm a man," Jordan asserts. "I don't gotta defend my manly choice."

"What's wrong with normal strawberry?" Abel asks as he spoons an entire clump of strawberry gelato into his mouth.

"Nothin'. You just not manly," Jordan jokes.

"I can live with dat," Abel sighs. "There's no perks to bein' a man in society no more."

"Oh shut up," Alex bites into her cupcake.

They all join me and lean on the storefront overlooking the traffic, cars, and people alike. We people watch as we all eat our respective treats. The sun begins to set on the bustling event of the street, the west side of the sky brimming still with a fiery orange and cooling into the expanding purple and blue. This is nice. I'd usually sit by my window every day after class and watch the sun drop from the sky, but it's definitely nicer to do it with them around.

I look down at my watch.

[Pizza Restaurant]
[Manhattan]
[7:20 p.m.]

I look up from my watch at Abel putting more pepper flakes on Alex's pizza slice. She massages her eyebrow with one hand and balls the other into a fist. She breathes in and out and loosens her curled hand. We shouldn't have sat them together in the booth.

"Now I can't eat that," she sighs calmly.

"Oh, Jordan will," he brushes her off.

"No, I won't," Jordan rejects the slice, "I'm full."

"I can't believe I ever missed you." Alex shakes her head slowly, looking at Abel.

"How many slices have you eaten?" I ask.

"Like two," he says.

"Lies," Abel says.

"How if there were eight slices in this pie?" Alex looks down at the table and starts counting, "Abel ate two. I ate one. There's this one that Abel messed up. Marcus ate one. You ate two … that's seven."

"There's one missing," I say.

"It's not missing," Abel says, "that implies it vanished. He just lyin'."

"Those are fightin' words," Jordan playfully threatens.

"You just usin' dat as an excuse to touch me," Abel shoots back.

"I'll eat the last slice." I reach across to Alex's side of the table to get the pizza.

"Stop it." Alex comes in between Jordan's and Abel's pawing in the middle of the table.

"You guys remember dollar slices?" I take a bite out of the slice.

"*Yesss,*" Alex singily screams.

"Yeah," Jordan says. "Shit's rare now. Dat shit is like three dollars now regular. Cheapest you'll find now is like a buck fif."

"I actually know a spot," Abel says. "It's a speakeasy. They serve drinks and shit, very expensive, but they don't card you and the pizza there a dollar."

"Yeah, but they're not the greasy and cheesy type of pizza, are they?" Alex asks.

"Def not," Abel says, "but you know … it's prolly the last stronghold."

"A speakeasy?" I ask.

"Yeah," Abel says, "it's a business behind a business."

"Is it a bar?" Alex asks.

"How do you know about it?"

"I just said they serve drinks," he answers Alex's question and then answers mine. "Some older comics brought me there. They've been doin' gigs in the city for years, so…"

"Shit, dat sounds cool," Jordan says. "Lemme know next time."

"Nah, it's dark in there," Abel says, "you might try to touch me."

I look down at my watch.

[Comedy Club]
[Manhattan]
[8:20 p.m.]

I look up from my watch.

"Put your hands together for … *AAAAbelll!*"

Clapping ensues as I look around at my surroundings. The room is pitch-black and even worse, the heavily lit set blinds my eyes, making it difficult to see the person next to me. I watch as Abel climbs out of the darkness and goes up to the stage, grabbing the mic with a smirk. The brick wall behind him juxtaposes his white vintage shirt with a cursing bear on it. He sits on the stool, one leg on the supporting beam and the other down on the floor. The spotlight illuminates him entirely while everything falls to dark.

With his chin pointing down, he gazes up. "I'm 'bout to offend a whole lotta y'all."

There we go. Of course … that is indeed his MO in nearly everything he's ever done. I've known him for years. Ever since the day I met him, I don't think he's gone a day without saying anything offensive. Even after not seeing him after all this time, I can guarantee—without a doubt—that at least once every day, he has made someone feel offended or, at the very least, uncomfortable.

Small chuckles emanate from the crowd as he pulls the mic closer to his face. I look over at Jordan to see his smirking, approving smile contrast with Alex shaking her head, lightly covering her face, mentally preparing for whatever Abel will say. Abel has been doing comedy ever since we were in high school. He'd go to open mics and even got paid to do a couple of shows, but I'd never think he'd actually make it into a profession. I mean, he doesn't take anything seriously, but I guess if there was any job where you could get paid to mess around … it'd be this one. He begins.

"I think this politically correct culture may have gone too far," he looks around the room, "we let a lot of people…," he turns his head side to side rapidly gauging the entire room, "become too bold in their identity."

The room falls silent. Well, what a way to set the tone.

"It's like the gay whites … imagine that …," he stands up from the stool, fixing the mic to his new height, and raising his voice while asking us with a smile, "imagine that … not only are you white and male … but you also gay as hell."

I hear a couple of chuckles; Alex's face has softened a little, still cautious to what Abel may say, while Jordan smiles profusely, awaiting whatever wild statement Abel may make to bring him to laughter. In that sense, Jordan is the best audience member you could possibly have.

"I—I mean you're safe from both sides."

The room flares in small bursts here and there. Without realization, my smirk had turned into a smile.

"Nah, I'm serious. They get away with everythin', and I'on even think it's like cuz they white men." He pauses, looks into the crowd and extends his fist, which is met by a white fist. "Y'know how y'all do. Shit, I'm trynna get away with some shit too."

The crowd laughs. I shake my head and sit back onto my chair as Abel sets the stool way behind him.

"No ... I don't think it's cuz of that. I really feel like," he pauses and shrugs, wispily whispering into the mic, "it's cuz they're gay."

At this point Jordan is laughing continuously. I can barely see him right next to me, but I can see the rows of white teeth. Next to him is Alex—her demeanor, while softened, is still serious and unchanged by Abel's words.

"White gay dudes will say all types of wild shit and no one will say anythin'." He twirls to one side, limp-handed with his hips sticking out flamboyantly. "I hate minorities."

He twirls to the other side impersonating a voice, "Ayy man that shit offensive."

He twirls again, "Wow, a homophobe. Typical."

The crowd laughs a considerable bit.

"Y'all heard the shit that happened in Pride?"

"Oh god," Alex says.

"Three gay dudes groped minors in the parade," Abel laughs. "They all looked like James Charles, so y'know…"

He smiles, holding in chuckles.

"They definitely gettin' off."

The crowd erupts in laughter.

"But for real tho, it's like a cop-out superpower," Abel continues amidst the laughter. He walks slowly on the stage side to side and shouts, "*Remember* … I think we should all remember … that Kevin Spacey sexually assaulted a young boy, *and when he got caught*, he came out."

Listening attentively to his cadence, I hear Abel begin to imitate Kevin Spacey's voice.

"He was like: 'I have something important to tell you.'" Abel pauses. His face holds in laughter, some busting through the seams of his smile. The crowd joins him in gasped laughs as he pushes forth, "You've prolly heard the news…"

A COMIC'S THESIS · 133

"Lord have mercy," Alex says.

"I'm gay," he breaks character.

I breathe out, chuckling as he breaks character, scrunching his face and waving his arms in an "oh I don't know" fashion. Jordan erupts in unison with the crowd. Alex, in contrast, has only promoted her face to a light smirk.

"Some people were like you're so brave for coming out … and I was like *huh*?" He scrunches his face in disbelief and disgust. "And people ask how the catholic church gets away with diddlin' lil kids."

Laughs erupt in the room with only a few people shaking their heads, shamefully smiling at Abel.

"The worst part was he came out unscathed … it's insane to think about." Abel reaches for the stool behind him and sits back down, touching his chest and swaying his head down to the stage. "My straight privilege still can't believe it."

"*Yeah!*" A man in the back whoops as the crowd howls with scattered laughs.

"Oh, a straight pride parade organizer is here," he laughs.

Alex laughs deeply as the crowd erupts behind us, people in the back patting the man on the shoulder.

"I'm not even allowed five feet within a school yard without people looking at me all weird and shit," Abel continues candidly.

He stops and puts the mic down as he laughs in unison with the crowd. He slaps the microphone down on his lap.

… *Thut thut thut* …

He brings the mic back up, sharply breathing his last laugh out, and continues, "I should've known. I've been taking the long way home … should've known."

He stands up again. "Minute I walk near a school yard," he proceeds to make another limp-handed gesture, walking flamboyantly around the stage. Alex snorts, trying hard not to laugh as Jordan reaches over gripping my shoulder, his body folded on itself as he vibrates on the spot. He sits back up and wipes a tear out of his eyes.

He sits back down on the stool, while the crowd laughs, and swigs a bit of water. "But now we know … gay is a good cop out for anything …"

He chuckles between words. "And I don't care what y'all say and when the PC mob comes for me … just know," he pauses and looks around and whispers slowly, "I've sucked a few dicks."

"*Ayoooooooo,*" Jordan shouts, as I place my hand on his shoulder, chuckling and shaking my head. "*'Bout gay as hell.*"

"Oh, shut the fuck up," Abel stands up again, dismissing Jordan's comment, swaying his arms up and down. "Just a few … just enough where I'm like not really gay, but like … I can avoid responsibility. I'm like one of those girls who's still a virgin cuz she's only had anal…"

The crowd laughs hysterically, while Alex huffs and opens her mouth in disbelief. She contorts her face and tenses it as she swings her head rapidly to see if me and Jordan are laughing. I immediately fake a concerned face and shake my head, making sure she sees my fake disapproval, while Jordan, as slow and as consumed as ever, just keeps laughing.

"Nah don't get me wrong y'all, I understand my privilege as a straight dude. I wake up every day without thinking about it."

…

The cackles and woos of the room begin to die out, Abel's somber tone bringing the audience to a still. It's always amazing to see how he does it. He always knew how to conduct

A COMIC'S THESIS · 135

his voice in a certain fashion, always knew what to say and how to get the reaction he wanted out of people.

You find the "appropriate" voice for certain situations and you can have it all. You can have people take you seriously or not at a whim. Even back in high school, he would get out of trouble as easily as he would get into it—and all he ever needed was his tongue.

"It's not easy being gay ... you have a lot of hard things thrown at you," he speaks in a slow pensive cadence, softening his face into a concerned gaze, "and you have to go through some shit ... just ... so you can have the minimum form of pleasures..."

I laugh, rubbing my brow with my thumb and pointer finger. The crowd awaits idly as he pauses, waiting for their realization. Obviously getting the joke, Alex snorts and, unable to hold it in, she bursts out laughing. Jordan looks at her chuckling, not fully understanding, but easily persuaded.

"*Wow.* That joke went over everyone's head." Abel slaps his knee while the crowd realizes and laughs.

"No, but seriously, it kinda sucks ... I'll stop ... I'll stop," he hiccups a laugh and just stares into the darkness, strange faces peering back at him. The wild hyena laughs simmer to a halt as Abel breathes in deeply, fixing the mic onto its stand, and then out. "It's hard to make jokes like dat."

"It's hard because nowadays you can't have nuance." He looks around the room solemnly.

I felt the energy in the room shift with Abel's voice, his serious introspective tone piercing the darkness of the crowd, rendering them completely still. Abel was always joking around. It was what he did. He made fun of everything. No matter how uncomfortable or how serious. It never mattered if bad things happened, he just laughed at it which, to his detriment, caused many around him, including myself, to see him as an insensitive idiot. Even after all these years of knowing him, even now, there's still a part of me that thinks that. It's hard to really know what he's thinking. I do think though, in reality, no one really feels his surroundings more than Abel does. No one sees and understands the world for what it is more than him. Jokes are the way he copes and—behind every joke, behind all the bullshit—there's always … introspection. It's the only way that you can make jokes like that.

He looks down and says, "You can't make fun of folks."

…

"And I'on really blame the weak ears of the masses … I don't,"—he scratches his nose, raising his shoulders slightly as he air quotes "weak"—"cuz I understand."

He stands up from the stool, grabs the mic, and walks to the very front of the stage, his tippy toes right at the edge, peering into the darkness. With a dark shadow on his face, looking down onto the crowd grinning, he continues, "There's too many neck-beard incels waiting. The state of the world doesn't allow nuance when there's so many ill-intended folks out there ready to use whatever you say for them to have an excuse to be bigoted."

…

Abel looks down at his shoes near the edge of the stage, his grin fading. "It's like dat in comedy … comedy is … full of bigots—or so Twitter says. I'on kno. Twitter says a lot of shit. Apparently, I'm a six, not a ten."

Some chuckles drown in the silence, including his own.

He holds the mic really close to his mouth, one hand in his pocket. "They might be right about some of 'em, at least from the folks I've met. Some people really use comedy as a visage to hide their true selves, and even if you're not serious about some of the things you joke about ... sometimes you're relegated as a helpful idiot because at the very least ... you at least enable it. It's a hard line to walk on."

...

"But I'm not sure, y'know. I don't think dat should stop us from sayin' controversial jokes, like people need to understand ... comedians are said to be operating at the forefront of what you can and cannot say in society," he wags his finger at the crowd nonchalantly, "and based on dat, we, the people, tune ourselves."

...

"Comedians, we—we not supposed to be taken seriously. Well. Dat's the idea at least." Abel raises his left eyebrow. "I don't know if I agree with it entirely."

Jordan and Alex are listening carefully at this point. Alex's face softens as she looks at me, pointing at Abel, surprised, as if the concept of compassion and empathy were foreign to him.

"It's not like a comedian ever said *'I'mma rape this bitch,'*" he shouts abruptly, filling the crowd with a mixture of awkward chuckles and gasps.

...

"And I was like *woah...*," he screams.

"I prolly shouldn't say dat shit," he continues nonchalantly, giving rise to multiple laughs around the room, except Alex, whose disappointed face sticks out like a sore thumb, juxtaposing the face of approval she wore a second ago.

"Y'feel me?" he says laughingly in amidst a sea of shushing laughter. "I'on know, I kinda just knew it wouldn't be the thing to say ... like even if I was a rapist ... I prolly wouldn't say that."

...

"I'd just do it," he smirks, "then come out as gay."

A big whoop and barrage of clapping ensues from the audience as Abel waves at the crowd.

"My name is Abel Sanchez, thank you so much y'all."

CHAPTER 9

BALLAD OF THE TIRED BRETHREN

ABEL
[Comedy Club]
[Manhattan]
[8:35 p.m.]

After my brilliant routine, everyone else paled like portrayals of Jesus. One by one, each comedian went after me receivin' mediocre applause, sounds reminiscent of a small booty twerkin'. The other comedians were ass, but that was the point. Put a pro amongst the noobies and you get a contrast. People stay and watch the entire duration of the show thinkin' that the ending will be the best, but nah. Unbeknownst to 'em all, the beginning is where it's at. It's a page straight from the Bronx Dominican fuckboy handbook, Section Two, Line Thirty-Two: treat 'em so well they become invested, then lower your effort, and deadass, they'll stay ... because they think you'll surprise 'em again ... because people want to believe good things only ever get better. They rarely do.

The dark comedy club gives nothin' but black silhouettes that laugh or chuckle at whatever is illuminated by the stage light. During the entire night, I sat next to Marcus, Jordan, and Alex. Throughout the entirety of the show, I'd glance occasionally as Marcus stared blankly at the stage completely mesmerized, as if ass was being flaunted in front of 'im. Well…

As the show progresses, the audience becomes drunk, cheering and laughin', enjoyin' themselves freely. At that point, a fart joke could make a drunk laugh, which is why puttin' the most trash comedians at the end works. Dummy smart move from the boss, in my opinion. Most comedy clubs have trash in the beginning and good at the end, but why waste people's good sense with trash, when you can give 'em that after a couple of drinks.

[9:48 p.m.]

Staying at our seats, the lights of the stage begin to brighten slowly but dimly. Everyone near us in the middle begins to stand up, stretchin' their legs, and headin' for the door. Some of the people in the back already left thirty minutes ago. The only remaining people were two grown men huddled together at the bar. The bartender warns 'em it's their last drink, but no amount of warnin' could quench their thirst, or loneliness for that matter.

It's a Thursday night, so the club closes earlier today than usual. Comedy has been on a downward spiral for years after comedians died or retired … shit just wasn't funny anymore. The New York comic scene, specifically, suffered the most. There were no more bald fucks makin' jokes surroundin' taboo subjects anymore. The comedy scene now consists of a bunch of effeminate men, myself included, and women. In fact, the whole line-up tonight was female, but me. Hence, people's disappointed look as they walk toward the door. I mean, let's be honest, when was the last time you laughed at a joke from a woman you ain't wanna fuck? Exactly.

"So, what did y'all think?" I ask, standin' up from the chair and stretchin' my legs.

"Everyone else was ass, but you dumb funny, bro." Jordan reaches over and slaps my back, hangin' his arms around my neck and bringin' me in. I can smell his deodorant, active in battle against the smells of the trenches. The deodorant is losing. I'd be tight as fuck if my shits smelled like dat. How he gets any sort of action is beyond me. Dat's prolly why he comes up to the Bronx to be honest.

Speaking of … I already know what she's gon' to say, but out of narcissistic curiosity and a need to fuck 'er night up, I ask anyways. "Alex, what did you think of my jokes?"

"You were 'ight, some raw jokes…," she admits, oh but wait for it, as she stiffens 'er face and perks 'er pointer finger up and shoves it in my face, "but that rape joke went too far."

I smirk. Coiling Alex has always been easy. After graduation, my taste for it only got deeper with the infrequencies of my doses. It's easy to manipulate passionate people. It's like a horny nigga goin' deep into an op's hood for coochie only to find out it's a set up. Shit's always a set up and, to an extent, he knows, but he's too horny to realize. That there is the weakness of being a man. In Alex's case, she just cares too much.

"So, the gay joke into the pedophilia was good, but the rape joke is where you tight?"

She breathes in and closes 'er eyes, joinin' 'er fingertips together and pressin' 'er joined fingers repeatedly against 'er mammoth sized forehead. "You not fu—messing with me tonight." She breathes out and just chuckles in defeat, shakin' 'er head.

Reader, you saw dat? I almost had 'er. She sits back on 'er chair and scowls at Jordan as he holds in a degenerate laugh, *sksksksk*'in' 'imself farther away from Alex's good graces. I smile profusely, slightly disappointed she ain't take the bait, but a reaction of defeat from time to time serves better than that of anger. Speaking of a continuous reaction of defeat: "Marcus, how 'bout you?"

"I could definitely see you going big, man." He looks over to the lit stage and nods at it. There's something weighin'im down. Throughout the entire day, he'd just be on and off. Bro's been in his bag since ... I'on even know. His face showed the type of pain one could utilize to get out the hood, like man give this nigga a mic or sum ... out here really sufferin' how Drake think he sufferin'. Brother man lookin' like he gettin' done dirty by some dirties. Not even A Boogie whole discography could save 'im.

"Dat's the plan," I say.

I look at Jordan and then at Alex, winkin' at 'im, givin' 'im the proverbial thumbs up and noddin' slowly. I go to 'im, pull 'im slightly to the side, dissimulatin' as if we lookin' at sum else. With a serious and solid face, makin' sure there's no hint of laughter, I tell 'im, "Bro she's been choosin' you all day. This is your moment. This is your time."

"Deadass?"

"Bro, I hung out with 'er for two years straight every day." I falsely reassure 'im. "She don't act like dat around anyone but you, gang."

"Ight bro, g'looks," he says with a smile on his face, as we turn around to see Alex grillin' us.

Reader, I know. I know. I'm foul, but ain't dat shit a lil funny? I know Alex and all I can say is Jordan. Not. Gettin'. Shit. Alex has always been a warm and touchy person. Maybe there is something there, but prolly not. I wanna see how that plays out tho, but also … I want some time alone with my emo brethren. Is "emo" a slur? I mean, what isn't nowadays? I'm not sorry if it is, reader. I hope I offended you. Jordan asks Alex if she's takin' the train and offers to walk her. She obliges, tho she's smart enough to know Jordan is nothin' more than a dog, so in a sense, she's technically walkin' im.

"We gon' head out." Jordan daps me up and brings me in close for the manliest of manly hugs, contrasted by the most sus of whispers, "You really think I got a chance bro?"

"Of course," I whisper. Nah.

"Be easy y'all and let me know when you guys get back home," Marcus says.

"Bro, I'm dangerous when I hop in these streets," Jordan clutches his wrist with one hand, his shrimp with the other, feet shoulder width apart, "they know my body out here."

"Man, shut yo bitch ass up and go home." Jordan has no bodies. In fact, he has nobody, hence his easy kills up in the Bronx and his desperate attempts with Alex. Alex daps Marcus, hesitantly daps me, then proceeds with Jordan out the door.

I turn to Marcus. "So—"

"I might head out too."

"Nah, sit yo dumbass down," I look at 'im sideways, as he gets up from his chair, "my son trynna put in work. You trynna cockblock?"

"Oh," he looks over to 'em leavin' together, "I could just take the take the long wa—"

"Man," I pat his arm, "let's talk for a bit."

"Abel," the owner calls out, wafting his chunky arm signalin' me to come over.

"Just wait." I nod at Marcus then walk toward the owner.

The owner is an old, fat, bearded fuck with white, curly hair. He always wore a goofy look on his face, one which I envy. The man looks comical and could run the whole place 'imself if he wanted just by standing on stage. Goofy as hell. He hands me an envelope full of cash—well, that shit better be cash.

"Thank you, boss."

"No problem." He points at the envelope and pats my shoulder. "Hey, put a little extra in there."

"Good, you already have too much." I smile and pat his chubs as he walks, broad based gait-like, into the back room behind the stage and disappears. Walkin' back to Marcus, I see J—the janitor—picking up the chairs and tables, placin 'em against the brick wall next to the stage. Out of everyone in the club, he's my favorite person.

"J!" I shout to get his attention.

"Heyhowyoudoin'," he places down a chair and takes off his headphones, "good?"

"I'm good, man, I'm good." I look around to see that everyone stragglin' around the bar had already called it for the night and, in their inconsiderate wake, left behind all type of shit and messes on the ground and tables. "You? I see you got a lot here."

"Yeah," he says disappointedly, "toomanymessypeople."

"You need some help?" I ask. "I might find me a dollar or two around here."

"NahI'mgood," he looks down at the ground and under the table, "ifyouhelpandIfindanythingIhaf'tosharewithyou."

"Fair enough," I chuckle. "Me and bro gon' be over there on the stage if you need any help."

I walk toward Marcus who had, by then, grabbed a stool and sat down right on stage to get out the way. The light still illuminatin' showed the ugliest of his features: a slant hairline, an unkept full beard, and a face in dire need of skincare. Luckily for 'im and unfortunately for me, I am one of the few witnesses to it. I grab a stool on the way over and sit down next to 'im. We sit there as J begins to take the floor apart, gettin' cups and half-drunk drinks from the table and takin' 'em to the bar, where the bartenders send 'em to be cleaned in the back. A deep silence, reminiscent of the sounds of slammin' doors and a single mother's realization that she'll have to raise the kid herself, permeates the room. It sits with us until it leaves with the boss and his lady friend as they wave goodbye at us and go out the door.

"So, this is how it is?" Marcus shakes his hand, pointing at the floor.

"Yessir." I stand up slightly and sit back down in my stool, adjustin' my sore ass—pause—on the stool.

"You just get paid to be yourself up here, huh?"

"Word too bro," I smile, "I just come in and talk shit."

...

"How's life?" I jump straight to the point, breakin' the silence.

"How did we get here?" He asks rapidly, almost as if I was the one to release the hammer he cocked, pause.

"We took the train here," I joke.

"No." He shakes his head.

"You been ambivalently present today."

"I'm asking about life," he says. "That's what you were asking."

"Hmm," I hum, "I was."

"What are you saying?" He smiles, confused.

"How's life?" I ask again.

"And I asked how did we get here," he says, like he gave me the answer of the year.

"How does dat answer mine?"

"That's the answer," he says blandly. "How did we get here?"

"Ahhh," I realize.

"Right."

"You not happy with life?" I ask.

"It's not even a matter of if I'm happy or not," he says, "I don't feel any way about it sometimes."

"Hmm," I tap my feet on the stage a bit. "What do you mean?"

"It's a lot," he says, shaking his head.

"Oh, I like a lot, y'know dat," I joke. "When have I ever been simple?"

"Never."

"Exactly."

...

"Nah," he yawns, "I don't know."

"You make any friends in Columbia?"

"Many," he says sarcastically.

"I see…," I say.

"It's hard to make friends there sometimes," he says.

"Why?"

"You go to NYU," he says, "you—"

"Went," I correct 'im. "I'm a proud dropout."

"Right, went," he says. "You know."

"Self-absorbed? Cheesy? Annoying?" I ask.

"A good chunk of them," Marcus says, scratching his leg as he extends 'em away from 'im, slightly kickin' his backpack, "but some of them are decent people."

"Yeah," I say, "you're just not compatible with 'em."

"Exactly."

"You ever just feel like they're removed when you talk to 'em?"

"What do you mean?" he asks.

"Like you see someone, you talk to 'em and you shake their hand, but you know it's not really *them*." I stand up off the stool slowly and put my hands in my pockets. I walk a bit on the stage. "It just all seems..."

"Fake?" he guesses.

"Nah," I pause to think of what word best to truly describe this dialectical Rorschach, this unoriginal individual, blandness incarnate, only to come up with nothin', "yeah, fake."

"Abel," he says blandly, "almost everyone at Columbia is putting on a fake persona."

"True, dat's college."

"Especially when you're a business major," he says.

I chuckle at dat. It's true. Those are the usual type of people that go into accounting and finance. Weirdly enough, it's never your average marketing major that acts fake. It's always accounting and finance.

"Bro, y'know how many people heard me the first time I got there my freshman year and started copying my accent," he continues.

I feel that. A lot. NYU kids from outside the city would always try to jack the culture and language, but still stay within the campus. They only wear uptowns, but never go uptown. It's wild to me tho the way they'd start talkin' different like they some study abroad kids trynna practice their

French in Paris. How you gon' use "deadass" correctly and still sound so … wrong. Deadass is the most versatile word in NYC vocabulary. You could say: he deadass farted; he farted, deadass; or deadass, he farted. It would all sound correct unless it came out the mouth of a suburban kid from Connecticut. Then, it just sounds off. I miss dat aspect of campus. They were my favorite part of the experience. Shit was always funny to hear 'em shout "yer" on campus, while drunk. Imagine fuckin' up one syllable, but anyways, what can you do when you get your personality from the internet. Reader, please be yourself—unless you're lame, then it's cool, be something else. Wear that hairstyle if you want too. It prolly looks less ghetto on you anyways.

"Yeah, I feel dat."

"Everyone wants to be something." He scratches his cheeks with his thumb and sits straight to stretch his spine.

"I mean," I pause and shrug my shoulders, "people change the way they speak and act mostly to fit in or to get sum, or to aspire to sum greater."

"Yeah," he sighs.

"Whose acceptance do you want?" I poke. Marcus's accent had changed not-so-subtly since high school.

"Well, that's different," he sighs.

"Is it tho?" I move my arms in question.

"Yeah, it is," he says blandly, "you talk about nuance in your comedy…"

"Right."

"So, you know," he continues, "when you and I are in college, you don't only represent yourself, you represent everyone that looks like you."

"Yeah," I concede, "dat's true."

"It's different," he says.

I nod as he continues.

"Over there, people either treat you like a commodity or like you don't belong. You're not seen as a student." He balls his fist and pulls on the top loop of his bag, stretchin' it. "You with a bunch of rich folks that have had everything handed to them. People that haven't done shit but the bare minimum in life other than going to school, studying, and being told what to do."

"Yeah," I agree. The worst part about it is dat they don't ever make the realization, so they truly think they got there with hard work alone. Nepotism is like holdin' your girl's vibrator at 'er coochie and then claimin' you made 'er cum. I mean ... true, but also not true.

"You're seen as a cultural commodity, a statistic to bolster the school's diversity," he continues, "so your place there is always questioned. So, you have to show them you *do* belong. You change your accent. You change your vernacular. You deal with the microaggressions."

He catches 'imself and breathes out, his upset face calmin' into complacency. "You deal with them trying to be your friends just so they can claim to be part of a culture that they can't ever relate to. I don't sound like this because I want to be 'cool' or 'accepted.' It's because I need to."

"Yeah." I listen attentively as Marcus speaks. This might be the first time in a while he's ever gotten to talk like this. It's often hard for Marcus to do dat. He just bottles everything inside into what I once thought was a bottomless pit. But Marcus, under all his silence and broodin' vibe, is really still the same kid I met at thirteen.

"I don't know. Everybody just got expectations of what you should be," he sighs in frustration, lettin' go of the top loop of his bag by his feet.

"Hmm." I suggest, "You could always go home, right?"

"With my aunt?"

"Never mind," I immediately say.

"Home feels like a step back sometimes too," he says.

"Why?" I ask.

"I don't know," he says, "I just go back, feel guilty dat I never visit, look at where I've been and where I'm at now. I don't wanna go back to the projects with my aunt or botherin' Jordan and his pops."

"I'm sure Jordan and his pops want you there."

"Yeah, I know," he says. "I don't know."

"You feel like if you go back, you'll end up staying there?" I ask. There's nothin' wrong with dat. I love the Bronx. I couldn't imagine livin' anywhere else. To me it would be a step down to go anywhere else.

"Nah," he sucks his teeth, "I just feel like I've changed, and I hate that shit."

...

"Marcus," I sigh, "You are who you are and no one can take that shit from you."

...

"Where you from and where you goin' is all a part of you," I say. "You just need folks to hold you down tho, and I'm sure you know dat."

...

"Is that why you don't link with us no more?"

"Nah," Marcus shakes his head, "I'm just busy all the time."

"Ayy man," I shoot back, "I'm busy all the time too, but I make time."

"You used to be a film student, remember?" he says.

"Dat's disrespectful," I laugh.

"Sheesh." I take in all Marcus's frustration and chuckle. He shakes his head and sucks his teeth and looks at me straight as I continue holdin' in laughs. "And here I thought you were in your bag over some dummy hoe who prolly hurts herself every time she sits down."

"I told you," he shakes his head, his face going soft, "you don't take shit seriously."

"I know how you feel bro," I say.

J had the entire floor bare by that moment and made his way to the closet to get a bucket and a mop. He had placed all the tables and chairs to the side.

I continue, "Code-switching, existential crisis, and all the bullshit ... what you feeling right now is normal, it's just change for the shit dat you gotta do."

"I just feel like I don't even know who *me* is." He straightens his back again and stands up from the stool. "I just feel lost."

"Right."

"It's weird that I have nothing figured out," he continues, "but people say I've matured."

"Some people misconstrue defeat for maturity."

...

I continue, "It ain't fair, but when has shit ever been. You just gotta find a balance that you comfortable with ... where you can be what you need to be and you can also be who you are unapologetically."

"Yeah."

"You're *you* brother. Your past and the shit that you goin' through now."

...

He laughs.

"What?"

"Oh my bad," he smirks, pushing me a slight bit, "Mr. Valedictorian."

"Mr. Valedictorian," I throw my arms forward, "and yet here I am, one year into this pro comedy shit. I already fucked two years of my life in college and nun of it was pussy."

"So that's why you left NYU, huh?" Marcus says half-jokingly.

I stand up from the stool, then sit back down again, shiftin' myself back. "Yeah, it was definitely that."

...

"How's your mom?"

"Y'know, she's got that little hookah machine now." I smirk. "She also screams all the time, so I think she's doing alright."

"Hookah machine?"

"It's what I call 'er nebulizer thingy," I say.

"Is she better?" he asks while shakin' his head at my joke.

"She—," I breathe in, "she as good as she can be."

"Hmm."

"Hmm indeed," I say.

"What about your dad?"

"He in Florida now." I breathe out and laugh. "Of all places … there. Florida."

"Florida?"

"Yeah moved down there 'bout a year ago," I scoff. Reader, I fuckin' hate Florida. It's nothing more than old people; retirement homes; amusement parks; bucket-headed hoes; Cuban and Colombian descendants of slave owners; and broke, behind-on-rent, New Yorkers who need a GoFundMe page to get back home after Spring Break.

"Why Florida?"

"I'on kno bro." I really don't. I could never understand it. Dominicans are whimsical creatures. Imagine workin' your entire life to arrive at a specific place to then want to immediately leave it thereafter. "You know how it is man ... Dominicans think movin' down to Florida gon' fix they problems."

"That's...," Marcus tries to find the right words to say, but comes out with nothin', "a lot."

"Meh," I say, "sometimes people need to feel like it's the environment and not their personal faults, y'know?"

"True."

"But ... that's how you know we ain't shit," I laugh hard, slappin' my knees. "This nigga moved to Florida of all places."

"You okay with that?" Marcus's chuckle dies out, now replaced by a face of concern.

"Nah yeah." I sniff and with a serious face and tone, I continue, "Last I heard, the Klan had burnt down his house."

"What?" But Marcus's worried face dissipates as he sees me soundlessly laughin'.

"Yeah, nah," I laugh. Marcus's worried face dissipates more. "Only thing I can do is laugh at it. It's actually kinda funny when you analyze it."

"That sounds more painful than funny."

"Pain is funny." I stand up from my stool and walk about the stage. "Back then, comedy was people deadass just dyin'. A piano would fall on someone as they leave the crib, shit like that."

I face the floor as I walk around the stage, looking at J, now at this time cleaning his mop and taking it to the back room where the custodian storage is at. "Man y'know how it is: we don't live in a place with therapy; we do what we can to cope. This is what I do, because if I make everything a joke, nothin' can hurt me. Nothin'."

J hurries to lock up the back room and motions us toward the door. "Alrighty'all, yougottagetout."

CHAPTER 10

THE AESTHETIC OF HARD TRUTHS

ALEX
[Outside the Comedy Club]
[Manhattan]
[9:52 p.m.]

The city street outside of the club is dark, dimly lit only by a few of the streetlights and signs. We walk down the street as nice residential buildings surround us. They almost look as if they're straight out of a NYC luxury apartment app. These have the underground garages with the blue light accented panels that say "parking." Some of them seem a bit old, but they're definitely nicer than the ones I'm accustomed to seeing in the outer boroughs. The views would definitely be nicer on the higher floors too.

"Bougie ass building." I point up ahead as we walk toward a pinstripe black-and-white-patterned overhang on top of a black-bordered, slightly tinted window. The wide window gives way to the inside: a waiting area consisting of chandeliers and leather seats and a Black Emperador Marble desk where the doorman sits.

"You'd be surprised how many of these are in deep Brooklyn now," Jordan remarks.

We see the avenue city lights pierce the night, cascading in all its colors, as we approach the corner of the block. The red, yellow, vibrant neons juxtapose the gray, dark, lonely streets we just walked. A breeze passes through the street, cooling the summer air. I love summer nights out. The city has a calming effect at ni—

"We should go to this speakeasy bar I know about."

So much for the calming effect at night. I mean the city never sleeps, never stops, and it definitely doesn't quiet down. For—

"You drank at the club, you wanna drink more?"

—some, the night is just getting started especially if you got the connects. There are still so many things to do.

"Oh my God, are you like ... my dad today? Always telling me what I can't and can do."

The people and conversations from the comedy club follow behind us to the corner of the street toward the avenue as groups from the audience scatter, a section of them standing behind us a little too closely and a little too loudly as we wait for the light. I look back at the loud, fumingly drunk girl surrounded by all her friends. You'd think they would get past their college days of being rambunctious. I mean, they look like they're in their mid-twenties at least.

"There's a party going on in the East Village if you guys wanna come."

She's loud.

"Nah, y'all have fun. I have stuff to do tomorrow early in the morning before work, so I'm just gonna head out."

"Alright man, bye Eric."

"Oh my god Eric, you're so lame!"

"See ya dude."

A man hugs everyone and then breaks from the group and heads up the avenue.

"C'mon Brett, you have to come. I'm small and I'm gonna need help carrying her around when she gets too drunk."

"Oh just let her fall from time to time, she might learn to stop drinking so much."

"That's rude!"

"I don't know if I should. It's a little late for me."

The group stands there momentarily, in the middle of the corner, trying to figure out each of its members' next moves.

"Just come, Brett. I won't be able to handle her by myself."

"It's 9:53 p.m., and I got work at eight tomorrow morning, but fine. I'll come for a bit. I get to shake ass to some ratchet music with y'all, wooo!"

"Yeah."

"Yesssss."

Ratchet? Ugh. People still use that word? The group heads down the avenue, whooping and dancing, some of the group bumping into strangers and objects as one of them, clearly the responsible one, promptly apologizes on her friend's behalf. They continue forth down the avenue repeating the motions. God, people have no home training they're so—

"Alex?" Jordan waves his hands in front of my face, turning around to see what I'm looking at. He looks toward the group, still bumping and apologizing their way down the avenue. "Them folks wild."

"Mhmm," I nod in agreement.

"They havin' a good time tho," he says.

"Hmm, no," I say in disagreement as I watch them kick a weird looking object with red lights in the distance.

"So, what's the vibe?" Jordan asks, licking his lips. "Like what's the move?"

"Boy, stop it. I'm going home." I look at him sideways. I close my eyes and breathe in the warm summer night pollution, slightly fresher than its daytime counterpart, but still all the while intoxicating. I open my eyes and look up and down the avenue, point to the other side where the street continues, and turn to Jordan. "But it's nice out, so let's walk for a bit before I head out."

"Bet. Bet. You lead the way." He smiles at me and takes out his phone and begins to type something into it. Jordan then, nonchalantly, looks around and presses his lips forward.

I deeply sigh. Abel, you bozo. I know you put him up to this. That's Jordan's signature "I'm gon' talk to shorty over there" look. If he thinks he's gonna be able to sweet talk me, then I feel sorry for him. Jordan looks like he was the hood heartthrob growing up, and of course he would be. Full lips, full eyebrows, nice eyes, and muscles would melt any girl. It would melt me too if it weren't for the fact that I'm well aware of his past and current fuckboy mannerisms.

"So, what were you and Abel whispering about?" I ask innocently.

"He was just helpin' me out with sum," he replies with a chuckling smile, as if his lips are holding a secret. He shifts his face to a more subtle smile. "I just had a sum on my shirt and he ain't wanna embarrass me."

"Wow." I raise my eyebrows.

"Yeah." He looks down to his phone and then back to me, wearing an ambivalently convinced yet unconvinced face that turns into a concerned one.

I nod.

"What?"

"No, I just—," I pause, "I've never seen him do anything like that."

"Oh." He looks down to his phone and at Abel's picture in a thumbnail.

"I've never seen him helping anyone out," I clarify, "unless he gets something out of it."

Jordan's eyes flutter slightly and dramatically as a look of realization washes over his face. He rubs his brow and lets out a defeated groan.

"What?" I act aloof.

Abel has done this so many times before to guys at NYU. He'd tell them something about how we grew up together, how we were practically siblings, how he's the best judge of character, and how he knows the cues for when I'm interested in a guy. He would continuously exaggerate almost every and any of my interactions and my minimal interest to gullible wanna-be suitors that come my way. In their defense, few of them knew Abel personally, but Jordan ... Jordan knows Abel. Why anyone would think he'd be helpful instead of chaotic is beyond me.

"I'm a meathead," he sighs, probably now understanding Abel's angle.

"How so?" I ask in an innocent voice, pushing the matter.

"Dickhead," he says, as he rubs the back of his neck and cracks it. He stares down at the screen and smiles.

"What?"

"You knew Abel was this big?" He changes the subject. He tilts his phone toward me to show me a video of Abel doing comedy with thousands of views and likes. He tilts his phone back toward him, taps the screen a bunch of times, and then puts his phone back in his pocket. "I ain't know he had it like dat."

"He's been doing it since high school," I say, moving on and preserving Jordan's dignity, "I'm not surprised."

He would always bother us to come every single time he had one of those amateur open mics after school. He always managed to get Marcus to go whenever Marcus was free. I went once our sophomore year in high school with Marcus. Y'know, you'd think someone with Abel's quick wit and lack of shame would be a natural at speaking in front of an audience, but no. He failed miserably in that show. Of course, this was when he was first starting out. It was so bad that until today, that first time was the last time. I never went again. Clearly, he kept at it.

"Didn't he ever invite you during high school?" I ask.

"I think he did once, but I had work after class usually." Jordan stops to think. "I would've gone tho. Support the kid and allat."

"Oh yeah, that's right. You were working all the time." I look down to my feet and move to the side, tiptoeing around the broken glass shards of a bottle. "He's definitely better now than he was back then."

"You've been there before?" Jordan looks and points behind us.

"Nah," I wave my hand at him, "but I went once to another one of his shows way back in high school. It was sophomore year."

"Sheesh. Sophomore year?" He shakes his head in astonishment. "I'on even remember shit like dat."

"Yeah, it's been a while."

We reach the corner of the street where the entrance to the building is indented into the quadrant. It was Manhattan City College, a small yet prestigious school.

Jordan stops and stares at the entrance. "Y'know, I was gon' go here."

"Really?"

"Yeah, I got into this, but…" He shakes his head disapprovingly.

"Why the one in Brooklyn over this?" This one was way better than the Brooklyn one, in my opinion. It's in the middle of everything and—

"Cuz … it's Brooklyn. Brooklyn's the best borough." Jordan turns to me, breaking his trance with the building and shrugs.

I visibly scoff at his comment. Okay? Brooklyn isn't even the best borough. It's definitely Queens, but I can't even have this conversation with Jordan—he wouldn't shut up and that would mess up the entire vibe of this calm night. The pecking order of the boroughs is a much-debated topic, the only consensus being that Staten Island is the worst.

"Didn't you get into NYU as well?" I ask.

"I did, yeah, but," he shakes his head, "they ain't give me a full ride, but the Excelsior program in Brooklyn College paid everythin' in full."

"I think it would've been fun to have us three there," I say. I'd definitely prefer having Jordan and Abel around over just Abel. Things would be less chaotic.

"Nah," he plainly says, rejecting the notion of hanging out with Abel and me, but probably mostly Abel.

"Hater." I lightly swat him in the arm, pushing him toward the building.

We cross the street onto the sidewalk. Jordan swerves into me, making way for a couple walking toward us.

"Yeah it's crazy how meticulous the coding and GPS tracking is in those robots around the city."

Robots?

"I wonder how Humanity got the funds to do it. Isn't it a startup?"

"I think the city forked over a bunch of money and they also got bought out."

The couple walks down the street past us to where we came from.

Ugh. We love public subsidies going to big corporations.

Approaching the next avenue, we watch as a smooth-edged, pill-shaped, robot crosses the streets on the opposite corner. It wheels itself onto the sidewalk, turns rapidly, and then stands still. Its spherical body opens something up and red lasers shoot out onto the street, scanning the entire sidewalk. I stop instinctively, but Jordan keeps walking. He stops and looks back at me, clueless.

"You ain't never seen these before?" Jordan asks, holding my hand and pulling me to the side to prevent me from stepping on bags of garbage. "These the new Humanity cleanin' robots."

"Thank you," I say.

I stare as a beam of red lasers simultaneously scans the floor, us, and out toward the end of the street, oscillating from the farthest to the nearest point. Whirring sounds start within the metallic body as the red light at the very top of the robot blinks twice, then stops momentarily. It blinks twice again, repeating the sequence.

"The light blinks twice cuz we here, two people on this street," he explains. "They clean offices and shit, but they sendin' these prototypes round the city now."

"Wow."

"Yup. Humanity's lil city-wide project. Just parts of Manhattan." Jordan looks at my confused and slightly interested face and continues, inching closer toward me. "Ight, so Humanity wanted to create a robot dat can scrub floors at a fraction of the cost. Automation of cleanin' jobs, basically."

"That sounds too good to be true." I walk toward the robot, still scanning the area, and touch its metallic body. "It scanned the street, but it's not moving?"

"Nah, it'll move when we pass it."

"How do you know so much about it?" I look at him, impressed.

"My dad…" He looks down as we walk past the robot and turn to face it, immediately beginning to vacuum and spin brush the sidewalk. "He's a worker at Amagone, and they just bought Humanity like a year ago. They use 'em to clean the campus."

"Oh." I keep staring at the robot's spinning brushes on the street as it vacuums the dirt from the ground, leaving a noticeably lighter streak on its path. I never knew Jordan's dad worked for Amagone, then again for as much as Jordan talks, he doesn't seem to ever say anything personal or substantial for that matter. I look over to Jordan as his face goes soft with a melancholic look on it.

"You okay?"

"Yeah," he switches his face quickly, "just thinkin' 'bout sum."

"I promise I won't go off on you and your pops for making a living," I joke, trying to lighten the mood. He knows how I feel about Amagone, how they've invaded my borough, how they've made it near impossible to live in it for most.

"Nah talk your shit, shorty," Jordan smiles, turning his head to look down Park Ave, "I hate 'em too."

"I don't necessarily hate them."

"I do," he says blandly. "You're more like obsessed."

"I mean it's confusing because they provide—"

"*Ahhhhhhhhhhhhhhhhhhhhhhhh*"

A scream resonates throughout the entire quadrant as our heads rapidly turn to the source of the scream in the middle of the street we had just walked. We stop in the middle of the crossing and walk back to the sidewalk. From a distance, we watch as the robot moves back and forth, stuck on something.

"*Help!*"

Jordan and I run over to the source of the scream to see a homeless woman draped in a garbage bag. She screams in pain as the hard brushes of the robot shreds pieces of her shoes and her pants. She kicks the machine away with her shredded shoes as she crawls back away from it. Jordan runs over and steps in front of the machine causing it to stop entirely, its bright red light blinking once.

I walk rapidly over to Jordan's side in front of the robot. It blinks twice.

He quickly turns around and kneels. He inspects her shoes and pants and sees there's no scratches. "You okay ma'am?"

She winces at Jordan's question, gathering her blanket and garbage bag quickly and balling them together as she crawls back against the concrete wall. She looks around anxiously and back at the machine past Jordan. Realization reaches her eyes as they begin to well. Closing her eyes into her blanket and garbage bag ball, she starts crying and wailing into it.

Jordan calmly takes out his wallet and takes out a singular twenty dollar bill and stuffs it in her hand. She grips it hard as she sobs deeply into her blanket and garbage bag ball, thanking Jordan profusely and reassuring that she is okay.

Instinctively, I take a step back, take my phone out, and snap a picture of the robot, Jordan, and the homeless lady in frame. Jordan turns around at the flash's notice to see me stand over them with my phone out. He looks at me with a bewildered face as he turns from me to the homeless lady and then back to me. He surprisingly and disappointingly shakes his head. He stands up, pushes the robot past the lady, and makes sure it continues on its course. The lady continues to cry as we stand over her.

"I'm sorry," Jordan says and walks away. "Let's go."

He walks quickly to the corner again. I look back at the lady and then down at my phone in front of me.

I think about the ponytail guy from the train this morning. Am I ... any different from him? No. Of course not. I'm different. I don't do it for me or for how people would perceive me. I care. I know I care. I know that the picture will justify the end though. I can share this and show what the robot did to this homeless lady.

"Why did you take dat picture?"

"I don't know," I say, "it was just my first thought."

"You see dat and dat was your first thought?"

"I just took a picture," I say in defense.

"Yeah, but you could've at least helped her first," Jordan says. "You just stood there and took a picture of 'er."

He's right.

We walk in silence down the avenue, another of those robots posted on the corner of a building. A light from the top of its head is projecting a small ad onto the outside wall of the building. We stop to look at it. The advertisement consists of people of all colors, of all creeds, looking happily out into the distance with a slogan that says: "Engineering and change for all." Under it is an Amagone logo, subtly placed.

Jordan scoffs.

We walk in silence a bit more, passing by smokers passing a blunt around in a circle in the middle of the street. We keep walking until he breaks the silence.

"Dat picture…"

"What?"

"Nah," he sighs. "It's whatever. I'on really care like dat."

"You okay?" I ask, hesitantly.

"'Engineerin' and change for all,'" he plays with the words in his mouth, uncertain of whether he believes it, "not for all, clearly."

"Yeah," I agree.

"It be like dat tho," Jordan says sadly. "It changes, yeah, but never for the folks who need it the most."

"Yeah." I look down at the ground.

"Dat picture is for your lil hashtag thing, right?"

"Yeah," I say hesitantly.

"I'on kno. I just feel like," he pauses, "sum gotta change."

"Yeah, I kinda know what you mean," I say.

"Nah," he softly says. "You don't, Alex."

"What do you mean?"

"I—" he stops.

We walk around a group of smokers outside of a club and slow our steps a little. He waits until we're a bit away from them to resume.

"I ain't trynna violate like dat cuz you do stuff," he says, "but you not livin' the lives of the people you advocate for."

"What do you mean?" I ask. "It's my community too."

He breathes in and out and with a calm voice says, "Alex you live in a decent house, your parents make decent enough money. You dumb smart, so you got a good scholarship for college. Yeah, you still gotta pay for some shit. It might be a lot sometimes, but people can't even make rent in the place they've always been at. I think what you do is a nice gesture, but at the end of the day it's just dat ... a gesture. There are few people out there really makin' shit better."

"I don't think that," I disagree. Shit has always been bleak in this city, but there's always people that want to help. "There are definitely people out there trying to do better by us."

"Like who? You? Like you just did right now? You think you gon' help with your lil projects and marches." Jordan looks at me sideways, his words carrying enough weight to hurt me. "You saw dat homeless lady, right? Me and mine are one or two more bad days away from dat."

There's a small pause in the air as he breathes in and out, containing himself.

He continues, "Even with the project, at the end of the day, they just gon' ride ya shit and market it for themselves, like Abel said. At the end of the day, the people most affected gon' be the one facin' consequences. You act as if you magically post dat picture that lady gon' be alright."

I listen to him speak.

"It—" He sighs, shakes his head, waves his hand nonchalantly, and shrugs his shoulders.

He has a point. I do live in a house with two parents, but it's still my community and my friends and my favorite businesses being pushed out. Maybe I'm okay in my circumstance, but I'm not okay with what's happening out there? I can't care about that? Why have such a defeatist mentality about it? That's all this day has been. Am I missing something? I don't know ... Maybe I don't deal with the consequences enough? Maybe I'm obsessive or in denial? But I would rather be that than complacent, and to feel like there's nothing I can do about it.

We walk silently till we reach the corner of a street. There's a station right next to us, but he just shakes his head and changes direction, nodding his head across the street and off the avenue we're walking on. We cross the street and walk to the next avenue to the next train station.

On the descending steps of the Queens-bound entrance, we say goodbye. He hugs me goodnight—smiling, wanting to say something—but stops himself. I give him a forced smile as he awkwardly walks away to the Brooklyn-bound entrance.

I go down the steps, swipe my MetroCard, and drag my feet to the middle of the platform, where a large panel of rotating advertisements shines brightly. I stare at it as it goes from moving purple and white accents to an advertisement for the white, egg-shaped robot with a bright red light we saw earlier. In the ad the robot is shown scrubbing a random New York City street, brushing away the dirt off the ground, and moving garbage bags to the side of its path. Bold white letters sit at the top: "Cleaning Humanity's messes."

I look closely at the garbage bags and eerily recall the homeless lady. I really shouldn't have taken that picture. I really regret that. I sit down on a nearby bench and look up at the displayed schedule: seven minutes. I sigh deeply, relaxing my tense shoulders and dropping them from my neck.

I should've really helped the woman instead. I mean, I didn't even realize she was there. At first, I just walked past her. No, now that I think about it, that's why Jordan moved me out the way ... to avoid stepping on her. I'm no different from that robot in that I captured a picture of—a picture to showcase a problem the city already know exists—but I failed to capture her ... humanity. Maybe Jordan and Abel are right. Maybe there's not much happening past awareness.

CHAPTER 11

YOU WON.

JORDAN
[Jordan's House]
[Brooklyn]
[11:30 p.m.]

I enter the key into the keyhole, turn it, unlock the door, open it, and enter. I close the door behind me, lock it, then take off my shoes and put my slippers on. I enter farther into the apartment, stumblin' on the raggedy ass shoes by the door. Dat shit gets me tight. Daddy never organizes 'em.

    I deeply sigh as I close my eyes in total darkness. Maybe I was a lil harsh on Alex. I should apologize next time I see 'er. I ain't have to say all dat. I could text—nah, nah. I'll do it in person.

    I catch the gleam of light comin' from under Daddy's door. It's kinda late for 'im to be awake. I walk slowly and knock on the door softly. I'on wanna wake 'im up. Maybe he just went to sleep and left the light on.

    "Jordan?"

    "Yeah, it's me."

I open the door to see Daddy layin' in bed, glasses on, readin' a bunch of papers. Bills sat neatly piled on his left. On his right, there's an envelope with purple accents.

"Why you up so late?" I ask.

"Wah mek yuh enter mi house at dis ungadly hour is di betta question." He slaps the envelope on the stack of papers, tryin' to hide it amongst the pile.

"Saw the gang," I reply.

"Das good. Marcus and dem, how are dey?"

"They doin' okay," I enter farther in the room, "Marcus asked 'bout you."

"Tell him tuh visit," he swipes his finger at me crazy, "practically raise di boy and he don't visit. Mi worried about 'im. Him nuh call me in weeks."

"Y'know how it is with 'im … always busy. Everythin' on his time," I sigh. I fold my arms as I lean back on the dresser right in front of 'im. "Alex is … same ol' same ol'. Abel had a comedy show. It was good."

"Comedy?"

"He tells jokes, we laugh, and he gets paid."

"Paid?" Daddy sighs. He takes off his glasses, leans back into his pillows, and smiles. "Yuh got any jokes yuhself suh yuh cya get paid too?"

"What? Me? You the one with jokes out here."

He chuckles slightly, turnin' his laugh into a cough. He clears his throat and reaches over for the water right next to 'im. The tremblin' glass nears his lip as he supports it stably with his other arm. He drinks it down slowly. Damn. Seein' your parents get old hurts. It makes *me* feel old.

"At mi age? Up inna stage?" He scrunches his face, putting the glass back down and rubbing his face. He stacks all the papers, bills, and the envelope with purple accents and puts it in the folder next to 'im. Is he trynna hide it from me? I done seen it already. There's nothin' to hide.

"Did we make it?"

"Mek what?"

"Daddy," I sigh. I move closer to 'im and sit in the chair next to his bed. "I already see di bills and di purple envelope."

"Boy, mind yuh bizn—"

"It is my bizniz," I sit forward in the chair, switchin' to patois, "I'm grown. I live here too. I also helped di lass few."

He looks at me fondly, smilin' for a few seconds.

"Wi dun," he says with disappointment, tiltin' his head back and massagin' his eyes and brow tiredly. "Wi kno dis wuz comin and mi want tuh wait till yuh finished school but…"

"Rent goin' up again? Utilities?"

"Yeah. Well no. Nuh dat," he sighs, rubbin' his eyes. "Developers stressin' Anya and Mildy to sell. Mildy wants tuh, Anya doesn't know, but dem old and tired, and it's a lot of money, so…"

The air itself stands still. I know what's comin' next. Daddy had lost his job 'bout a year ago. We've been livin' off savings, his severance package, and favors from Anya, one of the land ladies. Her and Daddy go way back, so she cut us some slack.

"…tired as well," he mumbles.

I can feel the pain in my old man's voice. I could see it and hear it all over 'im. I sniff loudly as my eyes well up, now lookin' deep into the light of the lampshade.

Daddy had worked all his life to give me everythin' I've ever needed. Like me, he was born in Brooklyn. He would go back to Jamaica in the summers and come back. Aside from the trips he made back to the island, he practically been here his whole life—this all he knows. He lived through the seventies, the eighties, the nineties, the circumstances dat made 'im into the man he is today. In his fifty-six years of life, he'd gon' through so much pain, and still, he stayed here. Brooklyn is his home.

Not to mention, this is *the* crib. This was where he first moved in when he got married to my mom, where he had me, and where he'd later mourn losin'er. This is where he dug his feet deeper, plantin' 'imself here to remember 'er. Daddy could've gon' back to Jamaica and lived with Grandma before her passin' too. Even after all dat, he stayed. This was where he raised me—and Marcus—a single father, alone, and always with a smile.

He keeps his eyes closed as he hands the folder to me, the purple accented envelope sticking out. I already know what it is. This is from the Department Against Homelessness.

"And this envelope with the purple design?"

"Sum money di city gives yuh when one is in our situation." He breathes in deeply and out. "We got maybe tree months, maybe four."

"Three months." Three months. Dat's all I got—three. I can still fix this. I can take a leave of absence and work full time, transition back part time, and yeah I'll finish late, but maybe we can stay here.

"I kno wah yur thinkin' … don't." He strains 'imself up from the bed, groanin' his way up to a sittin' position right in front of me. He wipes his eyes, stoppin' the wellin' of tears, and breathes out, "Boy, I worked mi whole life to gi yuh a future."

I sit farther back in the chair, scratchin' and rubbin' my jaw.

"Yuh'kno, I've made so many mistakes in my life and in mi yute," he continues, his tired eyes looking into my conscience. "Leavin' school a one ah dem."

I look into his eyes, seein' as the glimmer in 'em dies lil by lil until it becomes nothin'.

"Di odda, teachin' yuh patwa," he laughs, tryin' to make light of the situation, "yuh still sound so American. Even more dan mi."

I stare at the wall behind 'im, lookin' away from his tired eyes, unphased by his joke.

...

"I kno sum people in Connecticut." He places the check down.

Connecticut? He wants to move to Connecticut? You might as well have said we was movin' to Long Island or Staten Island cuz ... Connecticut?

"I always thought we'd be good." I look back at Daddy's eyes.

"Hmm." He reaches behind 'imself to the center of the bed and grabs the envelope, puttin' it in front of 'im. "This is an opportunity, boy. Wi cya leave, plan, yuh cya keep going to school, graduate, get a gud job, come right back 'ere if yuh desire."

...

He lowers the envelope to his lap. "Yuh education is nonnegotiable."

"Guh get some sleep," he looks at the clock: 11:47 p.m., "it's way past my bedtime."

I breathe out sharply, rubbin' my forehead. I stand up from the seat and walk toward the door, turning around. "Goodnight Daddy."

"Goodnight."

I walk down the hallways; years of walking had made it easy to navigate in the dark. I go into my room, sit on my bed, and look out the window. On the other side of the street, scaffolding stands tall behind a green, wooden construction wall, its face plastered with signs and city permits. I stand up, get closer to the window, and stare directly at the big banner displayed. It's dark, but the scant lights from the lamp posts on the street makes 'em easy enough to read:

"*Apartments coming soon in 2028.*"

I grab the blinds from each side of the window and shut 'em closed.

You won.

CHAPTER 12

SOCKS

MARCUS
[Marcus's Dorm]
[Manhattan]
[11:46 p.m.]

I open the door to the dorm and let it slam behind me. I pull a chair from the table and, tilting it farther into the middle of the living area, face it out toward the window overlooking the street and the park. I had left the window open when I left, which thankfully let the cool night air enter, evaporating the earlier summer day's heat. The slight movements of the leaves outside the window yield no rustling sound, all of it drowning in the silence of the near-empty streets and the building. There are rarely any students at all in the building during the summer, especially this late in August, making me one of the very few, if not the only one, on my floor. Everything was still in the summer, and I'd learn to enjoy that stillness. It definitely beats the constant sirens and music I used to hear when I was a kid.

I swing my bag from my back to the front and set it on my lap. Reaching in, I take out my yearbook, looking at the lightly faded yet still colorful cover, and set it within reach on the table. I reach into the bag again, picking up the photobook and laying it on top of the yearbook, leaving my socks inside. I throw the bag onto the sofa to my left.

I look at my high school yearbook, tracing the bizarre colors and figures on the cover, contrasted by the bland, black leather appearance of the photobook. I grab the yearbook and open it randomly. The page lands on the superlatives. "Most Likely to Succeed: Peter Yemelyan." "Most Likely to Run for President: Alexandria Serrano." "Cutest Couple: Ismael Rodriguez & Omar Zebedee." "Life of the Party: Amy Ostrowski." "Class Clown: Abel Sanchez."

Abel. I thought about what Abel had said at the comedy club. *Sometimes people misconstrue defeat for maturity. Some people get beat down by life and we call it growth.* I always think about how different things could've been if he'd come with me up here. He instead decided that he would much rather "be a genius amongst idiots than an idiot amongst geniuses" or something to that effect. He's right though. I *am* defeated. College and leaving did leave me lost and somewhat out of touch.

I sigh deeply and tiredly rub my eyes with my hands, elbows planted deeply into my knees. The whoosh of tires passes on the streets, breaking the deafening silence of the room. I open my red eyes and lean back into my chair as I stare at the photobook and the yearbook. I never meant to bring them with me when I went over to my aunt's to pick up socks. In fact, I actually didn't even remember having the photobook at all. I nearly forgot it even existed. It was just there collecting dust alongside a pile of other books and the yearbook. But I just sat there in bed looking at them for a while, figuring it wouldn't hurt to take them back with me. Now that I think about it ... didn't Daddy have it?

I slide the photobook from the table into my hands again. It's been years since I'd seen inside or made any additions into it. Of course, most of the additions made were never really by me. The photobook was a set of pictures detailing me growing up. My dad started it. He thought it would be nice to take pictures of it all. My dad grew up in the seventies Bronx when it was always on fire before moving to Brooklyn in the early eighties. With the fires and moving around, he'd lose a lot of photos, a lot of memories. Apparently, all of that turned him into the sentimental type. So, he made sure that when he had a kid, he'd give him something that he could look back to in the ways that he couldn't. He loved taking pictures, having pictures taken, capturing moments. He would always say it was important to know and "to remember your roots." It grounds us. I was never good at that. Ever since I was a little kid, I wanted to leave it all. Wash my hands of the past and just keep it pushing.

I firmly grasp the front cover. I flip the photobook open to the first picture ... This one here is ... my birth. There ... was a picture of my mother in labor as she screamed and a laughing man, my father, smiling at the camera while a bunch of doctors were in the back. I smirk and shake my head. He and Abel would definitely get along. This seems more sadistic to me than sentimental. She was apparently so angry, she wouldn't let him hold me for days after my birth. I don't blame her. I turn the page. The next picture juxtaposes the first. It's a picture of a bald man embracing a smiling woman in hospital garments, holding a newborn in her arms—me. Dillion, Jordan's dad, photographed that.

He was there for my birth with a four-month-old Jordan. My pops and Dillion were close friends and they are the reason Jordan and I met. Dillion and my dad grew up together after my dad moved to Brooklyn. I guess you could say, in a way, that Jordan and I are generational family friends.

I look at the next picture, one of my mom holding a chubby, smiling child—me. I take out the picture of my mom and me and flip to the back to see my mother's handwriting. I smirk. Even as a kid, even before Dillion told me, I knew it was hers because of how elegant it was. My mom was an elegant woman, there's no way it wasn't hers. Stereotypically, my father's letters were blocky. He would write his d's and p's almost identically, with the p's tail extending slightly—one penmanship quirk amongst many—that would make for many reading mistakes of those unfortunate enough to witness it. My mother's, on the other hand, was more fluid and cursive and filled with grace. I chuckle at the thought of my mother probably taking the pen away from his hand and him letting her write in his place.

Maybe I should visit them. I'm ashamed to admit I haven't visited them in a while ... since graduation. Sometimes I wonder how different everything would've been if they were still here. All I had to endure with my aunt. The neglect. The fights. The indifference. The coping. All of it just gone. It would've been different. Damn.

I turn a few pages to a picture of Dillion smiling, redirecting the shot of water behind a gushing fire hydrant on a summer street. Playing with water balloons behind him on the street were two bare-footed kids, Jordan and me.

Dillion. He's practically my second father. Jordan, by extension, my brother and friend. Dillion made sure to make me remember my parents, tell me stories, and to help me with everything I would ever need. He was the one who continued the photobook with every picture, every birthday, every Thanksgiving, every Christmas, every New Year's, every everything. If it weren't for him, I don't think I would've made it this far, especially living with my aunt. He stepped up and helped after—

I breathe out sharply, now realizing I had been leaning forward and holding my breath this entire time. I sit back and breathe in and out deeply, closing the photobook and looking at the plain cover.

Man ... Dillion, I'm sorry. I should've visited more before. Maybe I should go see him. Yeah, I just ... I wish I was as good a son to him as he is a father to me.

I look around the apartment, stand up from my chair, and walk around the living room. The sizable space suddenly seems cramped as I touch one side of the wall, take four steps and touch the other. I move the chair closer by the window after circling around the space of the apartment, pushing the table slightly forward with it. I sit down on the chair, leaning forward toward the window to smell the outside air.

The cold breeze stops, declaring the air stagnant, filling the room again with silence, only interrupted by the wispy leaves brushing against each other. I pick up the photobook, touching the cover again. I open it, skimming past the memories—every picture, every school award, every stepping stone—till the last page where there was a small stamp engraving: *"For my little boy, here's something to remind you what's important."*

It's just like Pops said this morning at the bodega: "Trying to move up is good, but don't lose sight of what's important."

My roots. It's hard to go back to your roots when you want to climb out of them, to branch out and grow into higher

SOCKS · 183

levels. How do you remember your roots if going back to them feels like a step back? I bet Abel would have a good answer to that. He always has something to say. Jordan would probably just say something like "You gotta straighten up bro. You a straight tree, not a gay one." Abel would probably make the joke better. Alex would just tell them to stop joking around and to stop being homophobic.

What's important? I huff a chuckle out amidst my tears. I missed them. What am I doing all this for?

Don't lose sight of what's important.

I grab my phone and go into the group chat: "Y'all trying to hang out at mine tomorrow?"

CHAPTER 13

A FRUITFUL MISFORTUNE

ABEL
[The Streets]
[The Bronx]
[12:01 a.m.]

The streets were desolate. No loudmouth, half-drunk Dominicans in front of the barbershop, no corner man trynna sell you some bum ass shirt, no shorties with the fatties walking about. The only place with the lights on is the twenty-four-hour laundromat. I walk past the dark buildings and stop in front of the laundromat, looking inside and taking in the quiet. I'd always assume this is what living in them small towns felt like ... only this would be ... all the time. Shieeet. Couldn't be me, deceased booty. The sounds of motorbikes boom in the distance. Ah, reader, dat's what I'm talkin'bout. My eyes weigh on me as I stare inside the laundromat and find it as lonely as the outside.

Imagine runnin' this shit for twenty-four hours, Mon to Fri. Like deadass, I'd be so tired. Fuck, I'm tired now. The empty laundromat consists of idle machines filled with clothes ... some dumb fuck treesh probably forgot to take them out. The floor, like always, seems sticky with dried black gunk dat would hug the soles of ya kicks with every step you take, like the hug of a clingy bitch with two generations worth of daddy issues. Not dat it's 'er fault for those daddy issues, but I mean ... y'know, unlike 'er father, she's clearly the clingy one. The oppressively hot air from the mornin' had left, leavin' behind a much cooler, gentle breeze.

Under the bluish-greenish lights, the gunk seems to have radioactive properties, and no matter how many times I've seen 'em sweep and mop, it never seems to fade. They never cleaned dat shit thoroughly. The gunk itself is ever changin', mimicking and imprintin' the sole of everyone who entered the laundromat onto the gray floor tile crevices, firmly holdin' their position until dry or someone else comes and steps on it. I rub my eyes and yawn deeply as I continue to scan the laundromat.

The foldin' benches are filled with loose singular socks, never to be paired again, and dried out dryin' sheets. The ceilin' fans spin, coolin' only the air itself, and the TVs watch one another attentively. You could at least turn the shit off if no one's in here. The walls are plastered with signs advertisin' the never-present low rates from five years ago, a twenty-four-hour service they sure dreaded, and free soap, which they stopped distributin' within three months of the laundromat's openin'. There was the Laundry Drop-Off service, with a dedicated schedule, for the "bougie" local Insta wannabe influencer hoes who couldn't be bothered to lower themselves to basic personal hygiene outside of what would get 'em paid in a hotel room. Or maybe it's for the hardworking moms who are tired of everyday life, in which case, do you sis.

The backdoor swings open and out comes a behemoth-ly ugly, short man with a large bag full of laundry. I guess he's the one in charge of the Drop-Off service. I watch as he plops the bag on top of a cart and pushes it in front of a washer machine. He opens the bag and begins to toss clothin' inside arbitrarily. How progressive of 'im. He looks into the bag and then stops, pausing to look deeply into it. I watch with heavy eyes as he digs his hand in and begins to shuffle clothing around, stoppin' midshuffle, with his hand deep in the bag. He looks up and outside, swayin' his head quickly to each side.

I duck instinctively and peer my head to see. I look around the street, still empty, and back into the laundromat, peekin' my head slightly past the windowsill. He pulls out, from the depths of sweat and nastiness, some dried-dookie laced red G-string and looks at it closely. I snap from my tired daze and watch as the man closely inspects the booty flakes on the panties. He closes his eyes and sighs deeply as he drops the panties in disgust. He held on to dat a lil too long for me, but man I'd be tight too, no funny shit, if I had to—nah. The man drops to his knees in front of the cart, sobbing, hands on his, ew, face. He stands up and, grabbing the collar of his shirt, wipes the tears from his eyes, only to be met with more streamin' down his face. Damn, homie prolly hate life. I ain't even mad at 'im. I'd break down working this bum ass shift too, but damn my nigga ... you—you couldn't have washed your hands first? The man starts to say something as he looks down at the red G-string, his lips exaggeratingly moving as muffled cries come from inside.

Quietly you can hear 'im sayin' repeatedly...

...

"One—"

...

"One more—"

...

"Just one more."

...

What the fuck? He looks at the clock behind 'im, next to the TV: 12:01 a.m. He grabs the coochie-sweated red panties and cries as he throws them back down onto the pile. Damn bro, just throw it in the wash. He looks back at the clock behind 'im again: 12:02 a.m. His face scrunches as he picks the panties up and throws 'em in the wash. There we go. It wasn't dat hard. He reaches back into the machine and takes it back out. He looks back at the clock and back to the panties and with tears streaming down his face—

And reader, forgive me, I've completely misread this situation.

He proceeds to swipe it slowly under his nose, deeply breathin' in the coochie stank of whatever dame too shameless and allows 'er brown-stained knickers, unmentionables ... what have you, be washed by someone else. Reader, I am stuck in the ghetto. You see what I'm talkin' bout? My interest battles my tiredness as I spring up, nearly to a jump, and watch 'im consumed in his guilty passion. He stops sniffin' and, with quaking eyelashes, he tilts his head so far backwards dat his nose nearly points at the TV behind 'im. His face stiffly contorts and then dissipates with relief and satisfaction as he trembles slowly, sighingly exhaling on the spot. Reader, I hope you like the vividness of it all. This man out here wylin', pollutin' the air of the Bronx even more with dat. Nah. Oh nah, I know you lyin'. The laundromat store manager has always been weird, but this ... I always wondered what time he on? And now I know. Damn, i'mma have to start washin' my clothes at home ... by hand. This shit is dastardly barbaric. My generation eat ass with no health insurance, but this ... this is tew much.

I can't believe this shit. I know I'm wylin'. Nah, I must be tired as hell. Yeah, dat's it. I'm tired. I always had an over-the-top imagination as a kid ... it has to be dat. I stand up rapidly as he shakes mesmerized. He quickly turns to the window and his satisfaction rapidly turns to fear upon eye contact. We stand and look at each other eye to eye, no homo, for too long. Reader, I feel extremely uncomfortable, but also if you think about it ... this is rather intimate and romantic, and I'm more than honored to be the one he shares this moment with, although very much lacking in consent from both our parts. He opens his mouth to speak while reaching out but stops as he looks down to his newly wet pants. I robotically face the street and walk away rapidly from the laundromat. *Ayooooo* ... this nigga deadass busted a gooey on 'imself. I look back at the laundromat as I keep walkin' forward. Nah. I'm tired as hell. I must've not seen dat right. There's no way this man really out here sniffin' doodoo. As I turn the corner abruptly—"Yo, what the fuck."

"My fault, big dawg," a familiar voice bumps into me.

My eyes adjust slightly to the dark as I step back and recognize the figure. "Rauli?"

"Yeah," he sees my tired and confused face, "you good?"

"Yeah nah," I look back down the street toward the laundromat with a blank stare, "I'm just..." My eyes in the dark are slowly adjustin' themselves to Rauli. "What you—what you doin' here ... now?"

"I just … can't sleep…," he looks at the laundromat's direction as well, "you good?"

"Trynna get home." I scrunch my face, look back at Rauli and away from the laundromat. "Whatchu doing out here? It's late as hell."

"I just told you. Y'know I got insomnia," he reminds me.

"Hmm, so you out for a walk or sum?"

"Yeah shit … but … y'know … and yeah … so."

Fuck, I'm tired. I ain't get nun of what he was sayin'. I blink and see the two bags he's holding in each hand and filling in the context. "So you can't sleep, so you just doin' laundry?"

"Yeah … do … laundry."

"You wylin'? Right now, right now?"

"Yeah…" I see Rauli's mouth move silently as he slightly flails the two bags.

He closes his mouth and waits for me to respond with a puzzled look.

"Hmm." I ain't get none of dat. I look back at the laundromat. There's no way I saw dat right? I mean I can barely hear Rauli right now. Maybe I'm tweakin'? I'm just tired, but imagine tho. Imagine. I snort out a chuckle and then face Rauli, whose face is now holding a faint smile.

"Man, you gone," he jokes. "Go to sleep."

"Yeah, I'mma just catch you at the shop."

I walk around Rauli, givin' 'im a pound instead of a dap, seeing as his hands are occupied and allat. I give 'im a final nod and see 'im disappear 'round the corner.

I continue walkin' slowly down the street, thinking about the laundromat worker—or is he the owner? Did I really see dat? This gotta be one of those fetishes them sexually repressed folks be havin'. Ain't he Muslim or sum … do them folks get any action? I'on kno, but ... man, dat's crazy. This man was out here bargainin' with 'imself talkin' 'bout "one last time" ... you mean to tell me there was multiple times ... I mean ... there has to be. Yeah. This can't be the first time. There's no way this the first time. Damn. In fact, Rauli goin' to the laundromat right now ... I wonder if ...

I cross the street and pull out my keys to the building's front door. I look back at the corner and it hits me, the free laundromat machines dat Rauli gets ... I just smile. I look down at my keys in my hand as a bastard's deep chuckle comes out, a chuckle dat turns to a wild laughter.

Yo, Deadass?

CHAPTER 14

RASTA MON IN THE BRONX

JORDAN
[The Streets]
[The Bronx]
[12:38 p.m.]

I walk across the street and catch the eye of a man. He stands in front of the laundromat lookin' from the outside in. He nods slowly, turnin' his back toward the front of the laundromat as he looks around the busy street. People walk past 'im, lookin' at 'im crazy, and I'on blame 'em. Not dat there aren't white folks in the Bronx, nor dat their frequent appearance here is as rare as it used to be back then, but they are starin' more so cuz of what the fuck this man got on. Muhfucka got a loose dashiki patterned shirt and dreads dat look like pikes going down his back. He walks with a slight awkward swagger, dat seemed somewhat foreign to 'im, yet deep within 'im. He pulls from his cigarette, which as I get close and smell the air, now realize is some Reggie. He blows it up into the sky. Even if the shit's legal now, police still mob deep round these parts just to "ask" around.

I walk past 'im, grillin' im from head to toe. He looks straight at me and asks in a forced voice, "Wah Gwan. Yuh from round hear?"

"Huh?" I scrunch my face, taken aback by his accent.

"Yuh from around—"

"Nah, I heard you."

"Oh, that's a nice accent," he says.

Fuck was dat? Is this nigga Chet Hanks?

"Where's it from?"

"Don't you mean where am I from?"

"Oh," he looks up and with a small lil nod he pulls from his blunt and slightly hiccups, "yeah … you right."

The smoke reaches my nose. Damn, das dat za.

"Brooklyn," I answer as he gives a distant nod. I look up and down the street and start to inch away from 'im, but stop. Maybe he needs some directions. Is he lost? Maybe he trynna get to Yankee stadium? Nah he a lil too far for dat.

"Oh shit," he blows out the smoke and with heavy red eyes looks around, tiltin' his head to the side, "I got a lot of friends up in Brooklyn."

"Yeah," I look around and back to 'im, "you lost?"

He's def not from here. You could tell from his lame ass accent, his bitch made face, and dat whole Jamaican cosplay shit he got goin' on. Poor dude prolly don't even know who he is cuz he's too busy trynna be someone he ain't.

"Nah mon, it's all piss and luv," he goes again with his fake ass accent. Pullin' from the blunt and holdin' it in his lungs, he exhales. "I just rode the tren to the heights, danced a little in the street like the movie, and then walked here to discover a new neighborhood in this gret city. We still in the city, right?"

"Discovered?" I scrunch my face, lookin' around. Fuck he think he is? An explorer? Columbus? Dora?

"Yeah, I'm from Harlem. Love the history and culture, but it's been getting a little dull round there. It's not like it used to be. Just a Farmer Bob at every corner and Amagone buying up the little businesses. They bought this Jazz club where they play reggae on Tuesdays, but now—"

"Man, what?" I can't believe this. "You? You from Harlem?"

"Bro listen to me," he points his fingers at me, "I moved to Harlem when shit was really popping off ten years ago, but now it's just boring. Barely any locals left or da history or da culture."

"And yo what's good with dat accent?"

"Oh, mi fi spen mi winters living in Jamaica. I get really depressed in da cole. Cole world, ya'know. Really lakka da culture. I feel like it was just made for me y'know. Just like smoking weed and chillin' by da beach. I just took it and ran with it."

"Made for you?" I get closer to 'im. "Yo, get the fuck up outta here, my nigga."

You can't just take someone's culture and use dat shit and cosplay in it. It ain't for sale. Plus, Jamaican culture ain't 'bout the smokin' and chillin' on the beach. Jamaican culture is sacrifice and love of yourself and your people. It's hard work and dedication. It's a father doin' everythin' he can to give you what he never had.

"Whoa, mon." He raises his hands defensively.

"Ay, shut the fuck up with dat 'mon' shit. Like what's wrong with ya māthā? Shit is dumb stupid, bro. You can't be yourself? You out here on the Ave. on some bullshit. You're tired of

Harlem? *You the reason Harlem is like dat.* You pushin' folks out they shit. You gon' take my home from me? My identity? All so you can seem cool? You don't give a fuck 'bout me and my culture. Fuck outta here. Dick rider."

People around the avenue had peeked their heads out their windows to see the action, some of 'em already videotapin' what's happenin'.

"*Ayoo slap 'im big dawg.*"

We turn to the source of the suggestion to see it's someone on the fourth floor of a building.

He looks back down and steps back, noddin' slowly with a struck face, which rapidly turns to a confused pensive one, "Wait … what's māthā? Is that, like, Spanish?"

"What are—" I breathe in and out deeply, calmin' myself as to not cause a scene. I continue, "It's bangla for head, for your mental."

"*Ohhhh.*"

"But man fuck allat, dat's beside the point, you ain't listen to what I just said?"

"I just learned something new," he ignores me smilin', draggin' from his roach and noddin' at me with levity, "that's how we do it mon. We learn from one another. I'm gonna use that now."

"Man—"

"We need tuh wuk together."

"What?"

"Fight the power, mon." His fist extends in the air as he jerks it around.

I get up closer to his face and through my teeth say, "You *are* the power."

"Why are you being so mean?" He takes a step back. "I thought spreading love was the Brooklyn way."

A wild laugh comes from the side, soundin' similar to dat of a stalled car. Abel. Abel looks at me smilin', his leather book in hand writin' sum down. He closes his book, slings his backpack over and puts it in there.

"Now, Jordan, I know you not disrespectin' this lovely mon in my beautiful borough."

CHAPTER 15

IT'S A CRAZY STORY

ABEL
[Corner Bodega]
[El Bronx]
[12:23 p.m.—fifteen minutes earlier]

I write in my book the punchline for a joke, inspired by last night: "Addiction is always how we cope with our trauma. It's just a matter of finding an addiction that isn't shunned upon."

Dat's some good shit right there.

"You out here always writin' in dat shit, gang?"

Ya lil book.

After snoozin' the clock for three hours repeatedly, I decided to get up and go out. I hate waking up this late. I just be feelin' hella shlumped and by the time you trynna do shit, it's already the afternoon. I might as well stay in and just chill, but I get restless at home, and Marcus wants to see us again, which is good. I have some time now, so I'mma just chill in the Ave. instead of the crib, plus I miss the regular funny shit out in the streets. Got a show tomorrow and the day after dat, so I gotta go out and keep grindin', writin' new shit for the masses to laugh at but never learn from, so on days like these ... I go and chill with the local bums dat come standard with your average, local bodega. The sugar water of food deserts.

I come here to talk to the local fools, the ones dat give you the best advice stemmin' from mistakes and, well, only mistakes. They're filled with nothin' but unbridled wisdom, permeatin' through lineages, impossible of ever bein' lost in this overly complicated world, not because they know the way, but because they have no destination. You see, reader, a corner deli bum is a well of hood knowledge and history, a connoisseur of everyone's business, a champion of laziness within capitalistic standards, and the literal consequential representation of the education system in a decayin', dying empire. Here you can come to find all types of inspirations, after gorgin' honey buns and downin' red country clubs. So here I am with Josh and Leudy, the newest edition of bodega bums.

"Y'know me, Josh, I like my ink like I like ya moms." I close my joke book without looking up, caressin' the now old leather on the book.

"What?"

Fuck he talkin 'bout?

"Leudy, stop dick ridin' everythin' Josh says," I say, turnin' from Josh to Leudy.

Josh is twenty-seven years old, still livin' with his parents, which in this economy ... understandable. The problem is he not workin', and his bitch live with 'im in his childhood room. The ghetto. Imagine pipin' your girl where you used to play with your action figures. Next to 'im is Leudy, a still-impressionable twenty-one-year-old. Went to middle school with 'im, decent kid, just doesn't know what he wants to do with his life. So for now, Leudy is the prospect candidate dat will take Josh's post in front of the deli after Josh decides to do sum with his life … so technically he might have a chance after Josh dies. Oh and his pops is one of the barbers I frequent and faithfully remain loyal to.

"Yo, you think … Ayo ma," the misguided Josh says changin his tone, "dat shit hella fat. Dat thang thangin'."

Wild fat.

I turn around to see a woman come down the block our way, her quickenin' steps insuin' upon the unwarranted approach of the boys.

Ah, the fine art of catcallin'. Reader, this is good. If you're an ugly woman readin' this, this might be new to you. This is the great method of tryin' to catch a fish with no bait, no fishin' rod … and no hands, and of course, no brain. This is a beautiful moment. A culmination of years, nay, decades, nay, centuries of the oh so fabled "mythical" patriarchy workin' to the favors of *man*kind. There is nothin' more elegant, more refined, more nuanced than this art. It's equipped with all a man needs to shoo away any opportunity for coochie or a dignified life. And the event dat you and I, reader, will witness will serve true to the fable. On the offensive side, we have a twenty-seven-year-old, five-foot-ten degenerate with a patchy beard and a semi-tan complexion, followed by a midget, no dwarf—no sorry … little person, I say—at a mere skinny five-foot-three, who is far too ugly for me to describe to y'all. You welcome. On the other side … oh. She looks … familiar. A brown, big booty queen with booty shorts, heels, and those now generic, hoop earrings hoes online can't stop wearin' trynna mimic shorty and the sistas. If you're a woman readin' this, you prolly wearin' 'em right now, but I digress … dat ass bein' fat is the only important matter here.

I mean clearly it's the most important matter, considerin' the guys didn't even see 'er quickenin' 'er step to walk past us faster, but again ... besides the point. Let's see how this goes.

"Mami, lemme get ya number," he continues.

You got IG?

There is no catcallin' moment *ever* in catcallin' history dat did not have a dick rider pushing it forth, an echo dat fully backs the main catcaller and pushes 'im ... to greatness. Dat bein' said ... damn this is a good echo. I'mma have to get his card after this.

"No, issokay, issokay," she reassures 'em of their position in relation to 'er, "you're a dog. You beneath me. Fuck outta here."

"Woooow." The misguided Josh is taken aback. The insult, unlike the receiver, clearly penetrates. "I'm just trynna show you better thangs."

Bigga heights.

"You're a bum, bro. You and dat short nigga next to you always on the block." She stops to entertain 'im, turning around, booty jigglin' and clapping in the wind, as she signals at 'er body up and down. "Like do you not see me? You can't even touch me."

"Nah—"

"It's the catcallin' with no *job* for *meee*," she interrupts, turning around booty clappin' like she slammed a door shut—and in a way she did—, "and you trynna get this juicy ass pussy. Fuck outta here, bozo."

"Ayo nah," he gears up as she walks away, "*you* fuck outta here, your ass flaps slippin' from them shorts. You ugly anyways, hoe. Suck my dick."

Suck his dick!

"No. Suck *my* dick," she retorts perfectly. "Every time I pass down the Ave. y'all feenin for pussy."

True.

"Das why you sound like Dusty Locane, deep voiced ass bitch."

She continues to walk away payin'im no mind, which promps 'im to continue.

"Like nah bro, these hoes dumb disrespectful, like they don't even take compliments no more."

Ah reader, what a show. I continue to laugh, writin' down the occurrences in my journal.

"Fuck you laughin' at?" Josh picks up his saggin' pants, a universal motion, for men readyin' themselves to engage in fisticuffs. Lucky for me, I know Josh is just bluffin'.

"Bro, dat shit ever work for y'all? What you gain out of dat?" I ask while pointing at shortie's ass, which is indeed fat as fuck by the way. I gotta give 'em dat. I know the lil booty hoes readin' this gon' be tight, but man I'm right. Suck my dick. Argue with a squat rack. Take it personal. I continue, "This is some broke bum activities, y'feel me."

"Dat ass was fat," he says like I'm blind. "We just trynna let 'er know and she bein' mad disrespectful."

"Man." I look over to shorty walking away in the distance. Of course she knows dat. Shit ... even if I were blind the general clapping of booty would let me know. Deadass ... but dat booty lively. Shorty is blessed. Unfortunately for her, dat blessin' is more a detriment when the thirst buddies are around. She gon' have to pass through the barbershop too, where she'll have further unfortunate encounters with married men, men who have daughters ... men who should know better, but don't. I look back at 'em. "Disrespectful is talkin' to shorty like dat."

See ladies. Look at me standing up for the shorties of the world. I am indeed *woke*. We respect—I laugh wildly, snickering and snortin'. Ahem. I clear the throat of my inner voice. Alright, let's try this again. We respect women 'round here.

"Bro dat shit ain't even dat funny," Josh says as my internal actions seep into reality.

Not at all.

"Disrespectful even," he continues.

Deadass.

"Nah, just leave shorty be." I point at the booty now at a distance, walkin' 'er way past the crowd. She stops in the middle of the next block, still visible past the multitude of people. A loose strap from 'er heels flaps on the ground as she holds on the side of a wooden wall. She bends down to fix it, the booty displayed in 4K UHD to the entire neighborhood—the only veil of cover provided by a … skinny, red G-string.

My eyes widen. Nah. No way. Maybe. Nah. Actually, life's funny dat way. I look back at dumb and dumber as they look at their phones, sounds randomly blaring as they scroll through Instagram. I look back at 'er as she stands up and resumes walkin'. Imagine. Imagine. I know these two clowns wouldn't care if anythin', but it's funny to know dat they've no idea what they're goin' for. I mean it ain't dat hard to imagine it to be honest on some sucia shit.

"Ayo, y'all know 'er name?"

"Oh, so you interested now?"

Yeah … you trynna get dat ass too, huh?

"Nah, bro-bro, don't jack dat," I shake my head, "I'm just curious cuz she looks mad familiar."

"Her name?" he says pensively, "I'on kno. I see 'er around tho."

"She pass through here yesterday?" I ask.

"Yeah," he says matter of factly, "she had a ba—"

"Laundry bag with 'er?" I finish.

"Yeah," he says, "she had on a sundress too."

Daisies and dandelions.

"Dat's interestin'."

"I think she used to be from the Heights, but now she lives up here now. I see 'er with a couple of [redacted] from up the block." He signals down the street perpendicular to the one we're at.

The big steppas from down the block.

"Yeah them niggas," he continues as he scopes out more shorties across the street.

...

The Bronx is lost.

"Wait, lemme get this straight." I scrunch my face perplexed, my left hand to the side holdin' my journal and pen as my right hand sways in the air, resistin' to slap the dog shit out of 'em. "Y'all catcallin' the shorty dat hangs with [redacted] from up the block?"

"I mean ... I think she's one of the cousins of some dude in the group, so I'on kno if she fuckin' 'em like dat, but I mean yeah."

Yessir.

"The same [redacted] dat was beefin' with [redacted] in Harlem in the middle of the summer?" I continue.

"I mean—"

"The same [redacted] dat hospitalized [redacted] in Inwood?" I interrupt.

"Nah, they not even movin' like dat," Josh shakes his head, "those are rumors."

"The same [redacted] dat won first place in the NYC Scam Olympics over Brooklyn?"

Dat was a fun event.

"It was." I face Leudy with a smile then continue, "Y'all out here catcallin' the shorty dat's always wit'em? Family or not? Rumor or not?"

Damn ... he kinda right.

"You sherm ass niggas. Is the math not mathin'?" I question. "Y'all want beef, no halal, no kosher?"

"I mean when you put it like dat it sound—"

Shit is illogical.

"Fuck you mean 'when you put it like dat.'" I scrunch my face. "What other way is there to look at it?"

"Ight, relax cuz you odeein' right now. It ain't even dat serious."

Mad aggy for no reason.

"Y'all need to stop catcallin' these broads regardless of who they know, but especially if they know *someone* ... period," I lecture the youth. Well, they older than me, but if age was measured in intelligence, I'd be the most grown person in my generation. "Fuck y'all want 'er for anyways. If y'all want more STDs so bad, all y'all gotta do is trade sippy cups, bozos."

"Ight, watch your mouth cuz you actin' real frisky this afternoon. Ain't even gotta violate like dat."

Facts, you talkin' different.

"I can tell you ain't get your ass beat enough when you was comin' up." He leans back on the sticker-ridden wall of the bodega.

"Perks of bein' smart and funny," I say.

True true true.

"Don't y'all ever get tired bein' on the block doin' nothin'?" I ask. "Just doin' hella dumb shit all day?"

"Whatchu mean, bro? His pops teachin' us how to cut hair." Josh taps Leudy, who grins from ear to ear. "We just chillin' right now, for real."

My pops a good barber.

"True, your pops is the best of all three I've ever had." I concede the point.

"Pause."

Pause.

"Pause indeed," I concede again.

I look down to my phone and see the time: 12:33 p.m. I swing my bag over, open it, stuff my journal in, and swing it back on.

"You 'bout to be out?"

"Yeah," I sigh as I step slightly away from 'em, "be easy y'all and leave these broads be. Y'all too facially challenged to be doin' allat."

"Fuck you," Josh says.

Das why your hairline fucked up.

"Aye watch ya mouth lil Leudy, I technically pay for your lifestyle."

I walk away and go down the street to an open fire hydrant gushin' water out into the street. I wet my fingers on the gush and flick my water-drenched fingers on my face and neck. The wind swifts through the asthma-inducing air, barely coolin' the street, but dissipatin' the water off my face and neck.

I continue to walk down to the barbershop. Flaco and Rauli are standing outside. I approach them, dappin' Rauli first and then Flaco, always. It has to be done in dat order. It's disrespectful to dap Flaco wit his sweaty ass palms and then swing dat to anybody else. I rub my palms against my pants.

"Dimelo, to bien?"

"Tranquilo," Rauli nods slowly.

"Ahi e'tamo," Flaco says, his wifebeater curvin' into his concave chest.

IT'S A CRAZY STORY · 207

"Aren't those your friends over there?" Rauli says, while pointing across the street, my eyes followin' his finger.

I watch as an agitated, angry Jordan gets closer to Chris. Oh sorry. Allow me the pleasure of introducing you to Chris. Chris is a weed influencer. He smokes weed. Dat's it. Dat's his job. He smokes weed, he reviews the particular strain, and he just walks around the city lookin' for more experiences. He practically gets paid to do what most college students wish they could do for a living. Turns out, Chris is also a comedian. Who would've thought the highest person in the city would also try to do the funniest job in the city. He's trash at it, but he gives out free weed, so he's very popular with the other comics.

I watch Jordan scrunch up his face in either disgust, disbelief, or just plain annoyance. He definitely wouldn't mix well with Chris and his chameleon ass. First time I saw 'im 'round here he came with a bum ass Spanish accent and a viva Mexico shirt. Thought he was just an Albanian trynna learn Spanish, but no. Homie's from California and you wouldn't know dat because he's always changing it up. Today he definitely looks different from before. Maybe it's the shorts. Dat dashiki is not doin' 'im justice, but it's a wonderful choice for this weather.

I dap Rauli and wave at Flaco as I walk across the street mindin' traffic.

"You *are* the power," I hear Jordan say.

I laugh profusely at Jordan's flustered face. "Now Jordan, I know you not disrespectin' this lovely mon in my beautiful borough."

"Wah Gwan Abel," Chris says. "Mi friend here no like me."

"Yeah?" I interrogate playfully. "I can see dat."

"Ayo, you know 'im?" Jordan asks with a puzzled face.

"Yeah," I face Jordan, "this the High Explorer."

"Huh?"

"He walks around the city high and puts it on the Gram," I explain. "He comes through here from time to time."

"What?"

"What are you not gettin'?" I ask with a chuckling smile. "He smokes different types of weed all the way from Zaza 2.0 to Blue Dream to Jerk Chicken, while he walks around the city. How is dat hard to understand?"

"Das crazy," Jordan says defeatedly.

"I like this spot." Chris points at the laundromat.

Shit. I move to the side behind Chris' tall figure to not be so visible through the glass front. I peer inside and see a couple of people, but no panty sniffer. Maybe he's not here today after his long sniff—I mean—shift. I look up to Chris, dazed out his mind watchin' the local news on the TV from the outside. He exhales deeply. "It's getting crazier out there."

"Right," Jordan says dismissively as he looks up from his phone and then to me. "Aye, I'mma head out, but I'll catch you later."

"You not comin'?"

"I am comin'," he chuckles, "but in shorty, haha."

"What?"

"Why would I be here? To see you? I'mma go drop some dick off, bro," he says smugly, "get ya some pussy too, so you stop hatin'."

"You ain't see Marcus's message last night?" I ignore his comment.

"Nah." He checks his phone to see the messages. "What message?"

"Abel, I'm gon' head out now," Chris says. "Are there any cool places or businesses around here to see?"

IT'S A CRAZY STORY · 209

"I'on kno man—" I look around with my arms open, but then realize. "Ight. So, cross the street, keep walkin' down for like a block, then you gon' see two bums standin' on the corner at a bodega. Take a right on dat same bodega, but be nice to the community, go inside, spend some money, after you take dat right tho, you gon' come up on a house with mad heads on the porch, they some good people. They gon' get you right."

I know, reader. I know, but I kinda wanna see what would happen if I send 'im high to [redacted]. Plus, I'm sure he has a lot of weed on 'im, so why not share? It's either gonna be really bad, in which case, meh, or it can be really good, in which case, what's the harm?

"Alrighty then," he says and in his best Brooklyn accent as he waves us goodbye. "Jordan it was nice meetin' you bro. Be easy. Dipset."

"Suck my dick," Jordan says dismissively while scrollin' through his phone.

"Keep ya matta up, bro," he says without turnin' back. We both watch as he walks down the block some more, takin' a joint out of a Ziplock bag and lighting it with ease.

"I hate dat nigga, man."

"Relax, he's just doin' his job," I say.

"Where's he even goin'?" he says.

"To [redacted]," I say plainly with a slight sigh.

Jordan looks up from his phone with a playful, yet worried look. "Nah, you trynna get 'im jumped?"

"He'll be good," I reassure Jordan. "He got some weed on 'im and [redacted] sell some weed too. They could prolly swap."

Legally by the way. Just in case a cop is readin' this. I'm no snitch.

"Man, nah. Go get 'im."

"You the one dat hates," I chuckle, "you go."

"Wow, you really a menace," Jordan laughs worriedly, "I hope you right or else they gon' have 'im in the evenin' news."

"You seen the message?" I change the subject. "You trynna come through?"

"I'on kno cuz I've been dubbin'er these past few," he says. "I might lose 'er."

"Yeah, about dat … lemme ask you a question." I get closer to Jordan and swing my hand over 'im. I start walkin' toward the direction of the train. "Shorty you be messin wit—"

"Ayeee my friend," a loud voice sings from behind, "aaaye."

I look back slightly and match the familiar face to the voice—the dookie-laced panty sniffer. He reaches over to me with his soiled hands.

"Oh shit." I shake Jordan. "Run. Don't let 'im touch you."

Without question, Jordan runs alongside me, fear struck in his eyes as he speeds past me several feet. We cross the street and slow down slightly as we look back.

"Please don't tell my wife!"

"Yo what the fuck goin' on with 'im? Why we runnin'? We could dead get it if he want."

"I give you free machines!" He falls to his knees at the end of the street. "Please, it was the last time. Don't tell my wife!"

"Shit … What the fuck was dat?" Jordan asks.

"Let's go," I tell 'im.

"But I wanna—"

"Man fuck your booty flake sneaky link, bro," I breathe deeply, "you better stop fuckin with dat girl."

"Why?"

"I'll tell you on the way there," I wrap my arm around 'im and walk toward the train station, "it's a crazy story."

CHAPTER 16

BEFORE AND AFTER

ALEX
[Marcus's Dorm]
[Manhattan]
[12:45 p.m.]

I stand on the sidewalk looking out onto the park. It must be nice to take calm walks there in the mornings. It's probably very noisy with the parkway and the street sandwiching the park. Columbia always felt so out of place. A couple blocks and there's Harlem, but Columbia just always felt like its own little bubble. Even when I was coming over regularly, dreaming of going here, I'd always be amazed of how close, yet so removed it was from it all.

"Yo," a dull voice says behind me. I turn to see Marcus holding the building door open. "You here early."

"Yeah, I was having brunch today with some friends," I sigh as I turn around and enter the dorm building. "There's some cafés nearby here."

"Right." He daps me up and brings me in for a quick embrace. "You trynna enjoy these last few days before going back to the grind?"

"Yeah," I say. These last few summer days pass at twice the speed. The minute August ends, December comes rapidly, then we're all busy with school and our jobs, and it's goodbye for now until perhaps Thanksgiving or Christmas or New Year's. Of course, that's usually time we spend with family or working.

We walk up to the elevator and Marcus clicks the up button. The elevator automatically opens as we walk right inside it with no delay. It closes and begins to ascend.

"What floor do you live on?" I ask.

"Fifth floor. Corner dorm room."

"You have a corner dorm room?" I gasp.

"Yeah," he says nonchalantly. "It's alright."

He probably gets such a good view from there. I've never had a dorm and I don't think I ever will. I decided to stay home and commute to NYU. Though a much-wanted and flattering experience, I didn't feel as though getting a dorm would be a necessary expense. Given the choice to live on campus for a couple thousands a semester or just commuting for a couple hundred, I'd choose the latter every time.

The elevator door opens. We walk out and immediately turn left. The hallway is mundane with empty white walls and empty boards. It's summer, so there's probably nothing happening, anyways. I touch the wall as we walk down the hallway, finger tracing and slipping off the wall as we make a right and continue. He stops at the end of the hall at the last door and opens it, signaling me to go inside.

"Sorry for the mess," he says.

I enter the apartment as he closes the door behind him. He walks to the side and closes the door to his room. I, on the other hand, instinctively walk toward the light emanating through the windows into the living room, where generic campus furniture is tidily placed around. Yeah, what a mess, alright. There is an anime poster on the wall and a small table near the windows with chairs sitting on both sides of it. On the farthest wall to the left, there's a small sofa with two books on top. I walk toward the windows and look outside to see ongoing cars and dog walkers on the sidewalk.

"You want water or something?" he says, walking into the kitchen just behind us and opening the fridge.

"Yeah, let me get some water please." I stay staring out onto the street.

A slight breeze enters the apartment cooling my forehead. I grab a chair from the table and turn it outwardly toward the window. I sit back and am met with relief and a cold touch to my neck. I wince and turn around to see Marcus holding a cup of cold water, next to my neck.

"Thank you," I giggle. I grab it, sip from it, then set it on the table.

"You're welcome," he says as he also turns his seat outwardly toward the window. He sets his cup on the table and plops down, stretching his legs out as he slumps down the spine of the chair. He lets out a deep sigh.

"It's so hot," I say.

"Yeah, but at least up here it's a bit cooler," he says as he sips his water.

"You'd think it wouldn't since hot air rises," I say.

"Air probably bogged down by heavy particles," he sighs. "There's a lot of construction happening nearby."

"True."

We look outside the window, our eyes fixed, mesmerized by the trees brushing toward uptown. A cool breeze enters the room and we sigh at the same time. It's always been weird to have conversations with Marcus. It's hard to talk to him when he never shares how he's feeling or what's going on. Then again, as much as we spoke and had class together, we were always just friends glued together by Abel and our common disapproval of his bullshit. We were never that close. A lot of that was more so due to his walls, not mine. After all the years of knowing him, I think maybe only once or twice have we sat down alone and actually talked, whether it be about his parents or his aunt. He's not exactly the best at expressing himself.

I put my back against the chair, left arm resting on the table as I swig a bit of cold water. He does the same, picking his water up and putting it up to his forehead to feel the coolness. I look past him and over to the sofa on the far side of the room. The two books sit tidily on the sofa, a colorful one, which I recognize immediately to be our yearbook, and a smaller black book.

"Been thinking a lot about back then," he says, breaking the silence as he sees me eyeing the yearbook.

"Hmm." I nod, looking back outside. "What about?"

"You ever thought it would be like this?" he asks.

"Like what?"

"I don't know," he says with a perplexed look on his face. "Never mind. I don't know what I'm saying."

"I mean, you're clearly thinking about something," I say.

He raises his eyebrows with a face of "oh I don't know."

"Life is often not what we think it'll be like," I say. "We get fed lies that we have complete control over it."

"Hmm." He raises his head a bit, his chin pointing out the window.

"That we can do great things," I say. I think that's a lie worth believing in though.

"Yeah."

"Y'know, how's college been for you?" I ask. "We hung out yesterday, but I feel like you didn't really talk much."

He chuckles weirdly. "College is a strange place."

"I don't know, seems pretty nice to me," I joke as I look around the room and behind me to the kitchen. "A little bit more decoration here would be nice though."

"I like to keep things simple, minimal." Marcus looks around with me. "Plus I'm not trying to mess up the walls with too much tape and nails. They might charge me more."

"How is college strange?" I ask sincerely, getting back on topic.

"It just doesn't feel real at times," he says. "Nothing I do here seems to matter. Isn't the point of college to improve people's lives and perspectives? Give them a chance at being happy?"

"Hmm."

"Yet, I feel like I'm surrounded by rich meatheads and I'm not happy at all here," he continues. "Everything we thought life would be like as teens just ain't it now as an adult."

"Maybe you spend too much time up here."

"Yeah, I do." He twirls his cup in a circle, the watery condensation easing the motions of the cup. "Still doesn't change that though."

"True," I agree. Adulthood and college have an amazing PR team. It's even worse when you don't come from an exorbitantly rich family. The responsibilities of adulthood compound faster, even before you graduate. Especially in

Marcus's case where he doesn't return back home. I wonder how he's able to afford to stay here in the summers and winters in a single room for the entire time he's been here. Must be expensive.

"I been meaning to ask, but how do you even stay here?"

"How?"

"Yeah, like money-wise, how—"

"Ah. Just work and scholarship." He swigs the rest of water and puts the empty cup back down, and continues, "My scholarship covers virtually everything. I work during the semester, during winter break, spring—during all breaks really, and I just live here on campus wherever they allow me to."

"Isn't that expensive?" I ask.

"I manage," he says.

"You rarely go back home then?"

"Sometimes," he says plainly, crossing his arms in front of him.

It's weird to think about how Jordan and Marcus were raised together. They're so different at times … most times … all times, actually.

"You and Jordan are so different," I say.

"How?"

"He loves Brooklyn … a lot." I look at him wide eyed.

"Yeah," Marcus breathes out. "He wants to stay in Brooklyn. I want to leave it."

"Right—"

"We grew up together," he says. "But we're definitely different."

"I was just thinking that," I say.

"Y'know when we were kids, we'd argue about dumb shit all the time," he says with a smile and nod.

"I can't imagine you caring about anything enough to argue," I say.

Marcus has always been a roll-with-the-punches type of person, or at least that's my perception of him. He never cared about anything enough to get angry about it. He would much rather just shrug his shoulders or move on from the topic than try to change anyone's mind.

"Yeah," he looks at the sofa and jokingly says, "you should give me a bit of all that care you got."

"Yeah." I stand up from the chair and get closer to the window.

After last night, I don't know if I care in the right ways.

"How was going back home with him anyways?" He shakes his head.

"He—"

"He hit on you?" Marcus asks, correctly assuming.

"Let's just say Abel and I are going to need to have a little talk one day," I answer.

"Oh," he huffs air, mildly chuckling.

"He's a troublemaker for everyone involved," I say.

"That he is."

"Jordan is—" I pause, looking down at my sneakers as I rub my right sole against the carpet, "much more mature."

"Misconstrue... for maturity," he whispers nearly inaudibly.

"Huh."

"Nothing," he says. "I was just thinking of something."

"You talk to Jordan lately?" I ask curiously. Last night he seemed to have something weighing on him.

"Yeah, before we all met up yesterday." He scoots his seat a bit more away from the windows and toward me. "Why?"

"Last night, he just—" I pause again, unsure whether I should even mention it. Jordan and Marcus had grown up

BEFORE AND AFTER · 219

together, but I'm not necessarily sure of their dynamic. I proceed anyway. "He just seems like he's going through a rough time."

"Yeah," Marcus says, "I haven't been over to hi—ours in a while."

"I don't know what's going on with him, but you're practically his brother…"

"Hmm."

"You should talk to him," I suggest.

"I haven't been the best brother lately," Marcus sighs, "nor the best friend."

There's silence in the room. He stands up from the chair and brings his filtered water pitcher over. He fills my cup and his to the top, and then sets the pitcher down on the table. His legs go limp as he sits down, dropping his whole weight on to the chair. I sit back down. He sighs deeply.

"Y'know—" I begin to say.

"Hmm?" He turns and listens.

"I was really sad yesterday."

"Why?"

"Because…," I sigh, "sometimes I feel like I care and it's for nothing or that I care the wrong way."

He nods pensively. "You're thinking about what Abel and Jordan said when we were at the park?"

"Yeah," I say defeatedly, "I just felt bad … he just made me feel like what I'm doing doesn't matter, then last night—"

"What?"

"Something happened," I continue, "I just realized maybe they're right."

He looks at me attentively, nodding.

"I just—I just think that maybe I can make a difference," I say, "I see problems, and I think of solutions, or just ways to better it, but I don't know anymore."

"Right," he says.

"I just don't understand why everyone has such a defeatist look at things," I sip more of the now room temp water in my cup, "and maybe that's the problem. I—"

"He told me something ... last night," he says. "We talked for a bit."

"Who? Abel?"

"Yeah."

"I won't say what it is though. I don't know if he wants it to be known..."

"It's fine, don't tell me," I say, waving my hand at him as I put my cup down. I fear for whatever Abel has to say and wants no one to know.

"Nah, it's fine. That's not the point," he says, "I think he cares a lot about things too, but he's just—"

I wait for him to continue as he struggles to find the words to say.

"People cope with stuff in different ways." He shrugs his shoulders. "He throws jokes around. You do activist stuff. Jordan holds it all in and releases it all at once. I ... I don't know."

"Yeah," I sip more of my water, "he doesn't have to be so crass though."

"He doesn't," he smiles, "but that's Abel. He just laughs and belittles anything he can't deal with or take seriously."

"Sometimes I feel like I care too much too openly," I say, "but I never actually get to do as much good as I'd like."

"I don't think that's a bad thing," Marcus says, "we need more people like that. Yeah, intentions aren't everything, but you at least try. That's all we can do sometimes."

"Thank you." I smile.

"Can I see your project?" Marcus asks.

"Really?" I reach over to feel his forehead with the back of my hand. "Are you okay?"

"Stop," he moves my hand away, "I'm just a bit curious."

I pull out my phone and show him the Instagram page of my project.

"Wow, you have a lot of followers," he remarks as I pass him my phone.

He clicks on the most recent post and swipes through the pictures, seeing the before and after of a chicken spot that has come and gone.

"There's this really sad one about a Puerto Rican restaurant near Williamsburg that had been there for forty-five years," I say as he carefully reads the post, goes back to my main profile, and starts scrolling. "It's now a—"

"Wait," Marcus says, as he pauses and scrolls back up a little. He clicks on a post and swipes. "This is the coffee shop."

"Which one?" I lean over a bit more to see the screen better. "What coffee shop?"

"This one." He tilts it toward me, swiping from a bookstore to a dilapidated, closed storefront, to a newly designed and renovated café.

"Oh yeah, that's in your neighborhood," I say, "that one was actually sent to me on Twitter via the hashtag."

"Yeah," he says, "Jordan and I couldn't really remember what it was before."

"And that's why I do it."

"That's why you do it," he reaffirms.

"It's important to tell these stories so that the sentiments of what the places used to be are remembered," I say as he hands me back my phone, "and so people are aware of how the culture of the city is being erased and replaced by something more aesthetically pleasing."

Marcus sits pensively, just nodding at me.

"People from around Brooklyn actually messaged me after posting that," I say smiling, looking up at the ceiling. "They said they had fond memories of the place as a kid and were sad to see it go."

"Maybe Jordan could add the Jamaican spot he mentioned yesterday," he says. "Y'know, he wanted to work there for free."

"Really?"

"Yeah, as long as they stayed open," he continues.

Who would've thought the man who didn't want to work at a senior citizen's center because it was unpaid back in high school would want to volunteer at a Jamaican spot? Then again, he probably had hoped to get paid in food. I smile profusely thinking about it.

"Don't listen to the guys," he says. "I think this is a worthwhile endeavor. It helps bring awareness, it helps people remember, and it helps people recognize what used to be there. It's good."

"Y'know you say you're not a good friend, but you are."

He sniffs out rapidly, raising his eyebrows in slight disbelief at my statement.

"You are," I affirm. "You just got to be a bit more present."

"Yeah, I've been thinking a lot about my relationships and friendships," he says. "The importance of having and maintaining them."

"Hmm," I hum. "Is that why you invited us today?"

Marcus's phone rings. He immediately takes it out of his shorts, sighs, takes the call, and puts it on speaker.

"You ain't see my texts," Abel sucks his teeth, "dickhead."

"We outside," Jordan says through the phone.

"We been outside. I been textin' you" Abel says. "Come downstairs, ugly."

Marcus hangs up, sighingly chuckles, and stands up. "I'll be right back."

CHAPTER 17

A LATE REALIZATION

MARCUS
[Marcus's Dorm]
[Manhattan]
[1:02 p.m.]

I leave the apartment dorm and rapidly go down the stairs. I press the elevator button to call down the elevator and then go outside, my shaky hands on the doorknob.

"Yeah bro, booty flakes all on the panties," Abel says.

"Nah, I ain't fallin' for dat," Jordan says.

I look at them bewildered. I don't want to know, but apparently something on my face signals otherwise.

"Yo, Jordan out here tappin' dirty-booty-flake girls," Abel says.

"I really wish I would've stopped you before you said that," I say.

They both come in, door slamming behind us as we walk down the hall toward the elevator that had arrived by now. I press the up button and the elevator door opens.

"Nah," Jordan says. "So you tellin' me he was there sniffin' the shit out of some panties and you was just watchin'?"

We enter the elevator.

"Brethren, word to my everythin', he did dat," Abel says. "He dead nutted too."

"I want to ask, but I'm scared." I worriedly contort my face.

"Is Alex here?" Jordan ignores Abel.

"Yeah," I say. "She got here like fifteen minutes ago."

Abel taps Jordan. "So you gon' stop fuckin' with 'er?"

"After flakin' on 'er today," Jordan says. "She might not fuck with me no more man."

"I mean … she's used to flakes," he says as he shrugs his shoulders.

"She kinda uptight sometimes, so—" Jordan realizes what Abel just said. "Suck my dick. You prolly lyin' like you did last night. You really violated."

The elevator doors open on the fifth floor. We walk out of the elevator, turn left, and continue to walk toward my apartment.

"What do you mean?" Abel smirks. "So, you would two-time Alex and have both of 'em?"

"No."

"It's a cold world," I say plainly.

"I'd drop 'em all for Alex."

"Ew," Abel and I say in unison.

As we walk down the hallway after turning right, my door swings open and Alex peers her head out.

"I heard my name out there?" Alex interrogates. "What are you guys talking about?"

"Nah."

"Nothin'," Abel says.

"They just asked if you were here yet," I lie.

We enter the apartment, greet each other properly, exchanging daps and embraces.

"Lemme get some water," Jordan says.

I signal him to the top cabinet where the cups are. He walks over there. Meanwhile, Abel walks around the apartment admiring the fact that it's much better and bigger than his apartment, lamenting that he has to share the space with his mother and siblings. He opens my room door and enters unprovoked and without permission.

"Where's the drugs bro," he jokes as he rummages through my messy desk, papers dropping to the floor.

"Get out his room, bozo," Jordan shouts from the kitchen. "He ain't tell you to go in there."

"Clown," Alex says as Abel comes out of my room and into the living room.

"*Yooo*," Abel looks at the yearbook on the sofa and brings it up real close to his eyes. "I lost my shit just a few months after receiving it."

He sits down on the sofa, after moving the photobook to the side. He opens the yearbook, flipping through the pages rapidly. He's probably trying to find himself. Jordan walks over to the table and picks up the pitcher, pours some water in the cup, and immediately downs it.

"Thirsty?" Alex asks rhetorically.

"Not anymore," Jordan gasps after downing the whole cup.

Alex sits next to Abel as he smiles at his class clown picture.

"Good times," he says, fake panting and drying fake tears out of his eyes. "Good times."

Jordan sits down on the sofa next to Alex, grabbing the black photobook. He almost throws it to the far side of the sofa but keeps hold of it. With realization in his eyes

A LATE REALIZATION · 227

and a subtle smile, he looks up to me as he caresses it with his thumb.

"You had this?" he asks.

"Yeah," I say. "I picked it up yesterday."

"I've been lookin' for this for a minute," he says.

"What's dat?" Abel asks.

Jordan opens the photobook to a picture of me as a chubby baby, which lights up Alex's face, but scrambles Abel's.

"Why you look like dat?" Abel looks back down to the yearbook, turning the pages vigorously.

"You were so cute!" Alex screams as she rips the photobook from Jordan's hands and taps the photo almost as if she's trying to touch baby me.

"This is your photobook," Jordan says, quickly correcting himself. "Well, *our* photobook."

"Is this why you wanted to get together?" Alex asks.

"Yeah, I thought we—"

"*Ayoooo*, y'all remember Mr. Hampton," Abel interrupts as he points down at a picture of an overweight man with patterned baldness. "I heard he got fired for getting too close to the female students."

"*What*," Alex says surprised. "No way. He was always so nice."

I sigh, grabbing a chair from the table and swinging it in front of them. I sit down and watch them as Abel and Alex holler and jokingly insult Mr. Hampton's looks.

"I don't know why he wears dat."

"It's a nice tie."

"That tie 'bout g—" Abel stops himself.

"It's what?" Alex dares him.

"It's very expressive—" he says.

"Right."

"—of his fashion choices."

"Hmm."

"Very much a fashionable choice," he continues.

"Good," Alex pats his shoulder, "use your words."

"New York Fashion week material."

"Beautiful." Alex smiles.

"Nah, dat shit kinda gay," Jordan says, prompting Alex to roll her eyes and smack him with the photobook. "Batty boy."

"Guys—" I try to say.

"Fruit," Jordan says while getting pummeled by Alex.

I stand up from the chair and sit down next to Jordan as he manages to take the photobook from Alex's hand. She shakes her head then turns to Abel and examines the yearbook. Jordan looks at the cover of the photobook, closes his eyes, and smells it.

He opens it up and goes somewhere in the middle to a picture of Dillion, Jordan, and me on Jordan's ninth birthday. His late mother took that picture. She died a couple months after that. I watch Jordan turn the page to a picture of his mother hugging both of us. He breathes in and out deeply. We look at each other and nod silently and slowly as he looks back down at the picture. He touches the picture, caressing her face.

I want to tell Jordan that I want to come by next week before things get crazy again, but I can't find the words to say it. The words are so simple, yet it's hard to pull that Band-Aid off when it's been stuck there for a while.

"That's why your forehead looks like dat," Abel says.

I look up from the photobook and to the three of them. Pops's voice echoes in my head: "Don't lose sight of what's important." Looking at us now I realize it's important to keep your friends next to you. People to hold you down when things get confusing, to laugh with and talk to when life and expectations beat you, and who make the effort to understand you, even when they don't. I'm lucky. Sometimes we focus on the goals of life, and never about the important details along the way.

"Leave my forehead alone," Alex says. "She's just—"

I think about all the time I've lost, all the memories we could've made.

"Don't lose sight of what's important," I say. They all turn to me.

"What?" Alex looks over confused.

"Ahh my son in his bag," Abel says.

"I just want to say—"

That I'm sorry for not being there. I'm sorry for being a bad friend. But the words never come out. We should cherish every moment and every opportunity we have because…

EPILOGUE

#THEBOROUGHS

…you never know when our story will end.

[Allie's Room]
[Brooklyn]
[5:12 p.m.]

"Rebekah, we're gonna be late."
 "Oh … my god Allie, what time's the movie?" I look up.
 "It's at six."
 "And what time is it now?'
 "Five-thirteen."
 "Okay then why do we have to go now. We're right there, aren't we?"
 "Yeah, but I wanna walk around the neighborhood before we head to that new movie theater." Allie slings her hair up in a bun and continues to apply makeup, stopping halfway. "I'm so excited to see that new movie with—oh fuck, my pasta."
 I turn my head around, perplexed to see Allie sprinting out the room. "Wait. You want to leave, but you're making pasta?"

Her room floor, riddled with the multitonal clothing from days before, creates a trail surrounding her bed, leading back into her jungle foliage of a closet. The only thing that had any form of organization in her room was her vanity. Her brushes and palettes had their own space, meticulously arranged to her liking and usage. She peers her head back, supremely overlined duck lips forward with raised filled eyebrows, while putting a forkful of pasta next to her face.

"You want some?"

"Why are you making pasta when you were just rushing me?" I twirl my chair around entirely to see her playing a game of lava, tiptoeing on the visible hardwood floor, avoiding her clothing and suitcases, until she reaches her makeup station. "We're going to dinner with Brett, Ashley, and Erik at that new place in Bushwick ... or Williamsburg, anyways."

"Oooooh, I haven't gone to Williamsburg yet actually," she says completely ignoring why she was rushing me, "that'll be exciting."

"You've been here for a week already," I sigh, shaking my head in disappointment to the slurping sounds of pasta. I twirl my chair back to the station and continue to do my makeup. "What have you been doing? You haven't gone around, not even a little?"

"No, y'know I don't like going out in the city alone," she says nonchalantly. She sets her bowl of pasta down and picks up her makeup brush and continues to contour. "I want to buy clothes from these really nice boutiques for the NYC clothing haul I'm going to do for my YouTube channel, or maybe I should do vintage—"

"And let me guess ... you need me to go with you?"

"Yeah," she says in disgust, "and the train is still kinda gross to me, and like there's always homeless people sleeping there ... it's kinda sus, but I really want to try it out."

"Meh, you'll get used to it," a response that earns me a disgusted look from Allie. "Uber there then?"

"But I want to be like *The New Yorkers*," she dazzles her hands in front of her face and begins walking around the room, flamboyantly kicking her clothing on the floor left and right. "I want to play in the snow, take the train, go shopping, fall in love with a misguided local so I can show him the way, but most importantly, to live in Brooklyn—"

And that she did. Well, some of those things at least. More specifically ... she came here to live with me. Well ... technically, I'm living with her. Allie has just moved here from our hometown back in Ohio. She had lived her entire life there, but visited New York multiple times, falling in love with the musical summer vibes, the earthy autumn colors of Central Park, the white winter wonderland, and the flourishing spring that the city became. She had stayed with me before in my small apartment, but now she's here to stay. Well, not here, per say. Her makeup and fashion channel allowed her to afford the city and *this* new apartment. She wanted to live with me, but my little studio apartment didn't have enough "good vibes" for her. So, she got a two-bedroom apartment and, upon paying the fees for breaking my lease, she asked me to move in with her so she didn't feel alone. I had already lived in Brooklyn for almost two years working at a now-bought-out startup. Throughout that time, her visits became more frequent. I guess those YouTube and sponsorship checks pay well for her to be flying so much, but it made her fall in love with the city even more. As soon as she hit one million subscribers, she decided to surprise her fans with moving to New York. Very original.

"And also, I wanna do that as well, but I am behind on two videos—my moving to New York vlog and my clothing haul—so I really need you to come with me."

"Fine, but only for three percent of your ad revenue," I half-jokingly say. "Tomorrow's Saturday. We can go then."

"Wow, okay businesswoman," she chuckles and turns to me, "and about walking around the neighborhood?"

I sigh deeply. I already know she'll annoy me until she has her way, so I might as well skip that part. "Be ready in five so we can walk around a bit before the movie and—"

"Yes!" she screams and runs toward the kitchen with her half-eaten pasta.

"Don't forget to text Ashley, she's coming to see the movie with us ... too," I sigh lowly. "I'll just text her."

[Five Minutes Later]

We lock the door behind us, Allie's excited mood showing through her little skips. We walk out of the elevator, around the corner, and past the key-fob enabled electronic door. The cotton-candy colored sky flares with accents of orange, emanating from the setting sun in the distance. The November air is chilly but pleasant. This might actually be a decently warm winter. Allie reaches into her leather bag and takes out her phone, videoing the area as we walk toward the movie theater. I understand it's how she makes a living, but Jesus ... enjoy the area a little without having to take your phone out.

"I know the movie theater is this way but let's take the long way around," she requests.

"Sure."

We walk two blocks, going farther into Brooklyn. We come across my favorite café in the area. It has a mostly glass front with black borders surrounding it. The white floor tiles are placed to mismatch with black ones, all contrasting the marble counter in the back. It's recently been my favorite place to go and work. "This is *Café Moderno*."

"Oh wow is this like a Spanish café? That looks really nice." She peers inside, looking at the workers cleaning up. She turns her head and looks toward the door, under the "closed" sign to a purple accented sign right below a rainbow sticker and says, "What's this?"

"Oh … y'know the city has had a problem with homelessness," I explain, turning around to face the closed-off park, under renovation. "It actually got really bad these past two years."

"Oh wow. That's so sad," she presses her lips together and pouts, while taking a picture of the inside of Café Moderno then turns to me, "is there like an Instagram post explaining the problems?"

"You shared a post like that a couple days ago," I realize aloud. "It's actually how I know."

"Oh yeah," she says, "I forgot."

"Yeah." I look down to my bag, reaching for my phone to look at the time: 5:31 p.m. We're good on time, we can walk around a little bit. "Let's go, there's some really cool murals and graffiti I can show you."

"Oh where?" she perks up.

We walk farther up the block on our way and spot two young men and a much older man, what I assume to be their father, packing the back of a huge truck with their belongings. Allie puts her phone in her jacket pocket. Gripping her Prada tighter, she begins to step into me and starts to push me into the street. I keep steadfast in my place moving forward, clearly signaling to her that we are going to walk past these men. Jesus, just walk past them, they're not doing anything strange. Well other than moving at this time … Quite weird to move out this late, when the sun is setting.

The older man holds a teary eyed boy in an embrace.

"Stay in school and be gud. Keep yuh head up, okay?"

"I'm sorry I didn't visit as often."

The other boy turns back to the apartment.

"*Dat's all in the truck? I'm gon' bring the last stuff from inside.*"

The teary-eyed boy lets go of the old man from their embrace and turns to the other. "*I'll come up with you.*"

"Guh, … here. I (?) sehd (?) goodbye."

The boys wait till we walk past to walk back into their building. I catch a glimpse of their faces from the corner of my eyes. You can tell one of them has been really crying. The other boy has a glimmer in his eyes that dies there on the spot, little by little, until it becomes nothing. I understand what it's like to leave home, but for some reason, this feels different. It doesn't have an air of bittersweet adventure in it, but more so of defeat. The old man leans on the back of the van, pulling his hat down over his eyes.

"Was that a Jamaican accent?" Allie smiles.

"I think so."

"They sounded so cool … just like Drake." She takes out her phone again, checks herself to make sure her makeup is fine, and looks up to the cotton candy skies, pensively closing her eyes … daydreaming. "Ughh, Drake. He's the only one that I'd ever let … y'know? Oh and Michael B. Jordan."

"Right." I crumple my face while grabbing her arm and pulling her from walking into dog shit. She looks down then up, smiles at me graciously, and continues to be on her phone as we walk toward the end of the block. We turn left and continue walking until we reach an entire street filled with murals.

"Oh ... my god, Rebekah," her jaw drops as she hands me her phone and sprints toward a mural, "take a picture of me with this mural."

The mural is of a man with a big chain and a black beret, placing his hand forth as if he's showing off his manicure. Of course, he's not really showing off his nails, but his rings. Each ring with a letter on it is situated on every finger but his thumbs, spelling out "B-R-O-O-K-L-Y-N." Allie stands in front of the mural, in between the rings, pops her hips to the side, throws her butt back, and holds in her breath while I take the picture.

"Make sure to get my good angles," she screams.

I move around from different angles, taking the pictures until I see a message pop up on her phone and accidently click it. Shit. I gasp and tell her the time, "It's 5:42."

"Don't worry it's okay," she waves her hand, then placing them at her hips nonchalantly, "let's just keep taking pictures."

"No. The text is from Ashley. She's in line right now," I hold her phone up for her to see, "I alr—"

"Oh god, I forgot to text her."

"I already texted her." I hand Allie her phone back and start walking in the direction of the new movie theater.

Allie lags closely behind, unaccustomed to the speed that most New Yorkers develop. She'll get used to it. Looking down at her phone all the time doesn't help though.

We walk two blocks and back to our street. One block away, there stands a line to get into the movie. We walk toward the line but wait for the light to cross the street. Beside

#THEBOROUGHS · 237

us is an entrance to an over ground train station with an electronic advertisement on the overhead. A lady and her kids pass by as the screen pixelates and displays:

"*As per established NYC rent control guidelines, it is against the law for landlords to randomly increase your rent. If your landlord is randomly increasing your rent, please notify the NYC tenant phone line: (917) 555-RENT.*

Tenants have rights. We stand with you.

Sponsored by the NYC Department Against Homelessness."

I look at the purple-accented advertisement, the woman on it holding her kids in an embrace, smiling. Allie looks at me and then to where I'm looking as the digital screen pixelates again, now showing an advertisement for *The New Yorkers*.

"That show is *so* good. We should do a marathon before season six starts next week."

"I have work." I chuckle, looking back at the crosswalk to see cars stopped and the walking signal on the other side. "Let's go."

We arrive at the line to see a hand waving from amongst it. Ashley.

"Oh my god," a screech resounds from Allie as she runs toward Ashley, "I haven't seen you in so long."

"It's been long, yes." Ashley embraces Allie and opens her eyes wide, concerned, while looking at me. "Hey Rebekah, how are you guys?"

"I'm go—"

"I'm *so* excited to be here, starting this new chapter in my life." Allie takes her phone out and shows Ashley the pictures taken by the mural. "Look."

"Wow," she looks at her phone, "those are really nice, you should post them."

"Of course I'm going to post them."

She opens up various apps on her phone, editing her picture and, of course, fine-tuning her features. She's an influencer after all. She opens Instagram and begins to write her caption.

"So, how've you been?"

"I've been okay. One day at a time with work and everything."

"Yeah." Ashley shakes her head vigorously, rolling her head back trying hard to relate. Her parents were wealthy businesspeople and had left her an entire franchise to manage in lower Manhattan. Normally running an entire franchise would be a lot of work, but I've seen her work. All she does is hold meetings with people who already have decided to do business with her. The deal is already sealed, it's just all a formality. "I get it."

"Yeah." I lift the corner of my mouth.

Allie shows me her phone as she edits the picture. "Highlights up or down?"

"Slightly down," I respond, as she keeps going at her phone.

"Hey," Ashley tilts her head curiously, "did you ever go to the women's march a couple months ago?"

"Women's march?" I actually remember that day. We went to this random comedy club and I had to sleep over at Ashley's after tiring myself out dragging her up the stairs to her apartment. Next time she gets that fumingly drunk, I'll just leave her at the bottom of the stairs.

"Yeah," she nods continuously, pointing her chin in front of her, "my friends went. I saw the vagina-shaped pictures, it was like … really powerful, but they met really strange people."

#THEBOROUGHS · 239

"Right, I'm sure they did." I inch forward in the line, filling the gap as it moves forward.

"There's a lot of people here to see this movie," Ashley comments, "is it really that popular?"

"This movie is gonna be *so* good." Allie looks up from her phone, slowly raising her head dramatically from editing her favorite picture, and looks at Ashley and me. "Imagine a movie showing social issues being confronted by girl power, veiled in irony, action, and a great tribute to cinema, the arts, and the world—*The Liberator: Growing Knee Pain*."

Ashley nods awkwardly, unable to answer that with anything substantial. "I hear it has a lot of action."

"It is indeed an action film," I say.

"What are you guys doing next week?" Ashley asks.

Allie ignores Ashley as she continues to edit her picture. I peek at her phone and watch as she Facetunes the blemishes off her face. Hours spent on makeup and Facetune had rendered her unidentintical to some of her other Instagram pictures and, well, reality.

"I'm probably gonna be working, y'know, at my job," I say.

"You work hard. Take some sick leaves and come with me to this new thing they're setting up under the Brooklyn Bridge. You can rent out these nice little minivans and you can kinda like…," she pauses and thinks for a moment, "kinda like you're homeless, but not really."

"I don't think 'homeless' would be the word for that experience."

"Right, but you know what I mean."

"Right, but how—"

"It's this new attraction that they put up," she asserts, "you basically sleep in this really decked out mini-van with lights and it's very aesthetically pleasing. It's by the water, and the city lights, and it's still pretty warm."

"*Ooooo*," Allie whoops as she looks up from her phone. "I'm in. Let me know when next week."

"You guys have fun with that," I respond.

"I'll send you the thing on your—"

"Okay, I'm almost done." Allie proudly shows us her before-and-after picture edits, opens up Instagram again, and looks up to the sky. "Ughh I don't know what to put as a caption."

"Does it matter?" Ashley asks innocently.

"That's a dumb question," Allie retorts passive-aggressively as she looks down and cups her phone in her hands, fidgeting and twiddling her thumbs over the screen. Of course it doesn't matter, but it's Allie. She makes a big deal over the small stuff and disregards the big ones. She looks up and to us both. "Of course it matters. Everything you do needs to send a message."

"Just … write about how … excited you are to be here," I suggest, uninterested.

"Yes," she says singly, grabbing my arm as she runs in place excitedly, "I'm *so* happy to be here. Okay, I'll do that."

She begins to write up her feelings.

Without realizing, we had inched our way to the door of the cinema, the line dispersing as people began getting situated and walking to theaters. Before entering through the door, Allie shoves her phone in my face. "You think this is good?"

"So excited to start this new chapter in my new city. Meet your new #thenewyorkers," I read out loud.

"Hmmm, it's missing something." She takes her phone back and looks up, puffing her cheeks with air, clearly unsatisfied.

"Maybe my voice made it sound boring?"

"That hashtag seems very basic," Ashley suggests, "why not—"

Allie shushes Ashley. We stare at her as she stares pensively at what she'd describe as nothing more than a simple masterpiece. "I know the perfect hashtag. I've seen it around the city."

"What is it?"

She turns her phone around to a picture uploaded twelve seconds ago, already with twenty likes. It's her in front of the mural. Her caption says:

So excited to start this new chapter in my new city.
#theboroughs

ACKNOWLEDGMENT

If you're reading this then that means you've reached the end. I hope you enjoyed it.

Gratitude is a necessary part of growth. It grounds you and allows you to work with the bits that you may have. Looking back, the happiest moments of my life have been when I thought of all the things I've had and not the things I lacked. Throughout the writing process, unfortunately, I felt like I had few real supporters, and perhaps none at all. I felt like no one would care about my work. I felt like few people would care about what I had to say. I felt alone.

I announced I was writing a book, and many liked my post, some messaged me, but very few actually pre-ordered or donated. I was slightly discouraged, but I was so grateful to the few who had given me words of affirmation and donated however small amount they could toward me. I want to thank those people as listed below whether they helped through interviews, donation, or inspiration. Thank you.

Cristian Vargas
Isabella Tran
Ethan Strauther

Aylin Perez
Arileyda V. Baez
Jared Candelaria

Jason Pichardo	Ohilda Holguin
Ojany Vargas	Eric Koester
Anilkumar Khemlani	Helen Field
Kenju Gibbs	Maria Baez
Carolina Baez	Rosa Baez
Yuberki Baez	Kisha Chandler
Felix Levine	LaReya Brown
Karina Agbisit	Sam Jensen
Caleb Amanfu	Davonte T. Williams
Sierra Penrod	George Sanchez
Tiffany Henry	Camryn Privette